500
Words, Phrases, Idioms
for the
TOEFL® iBT
plus Typing Strategies

by

Bruce Stirling

TOEFL® is a registered trademark of Educational Testing Services (ETS®), Princeton, New Jersey, USA. The strategies and test samples in this text were created and designed exclusively by the author Bruce Stirling. This publication is not endorsed or approved by ETS.

For permission to use material from this text or the CDs, please forward your request to info@novapress.net.

ISBN 10: 1-889057-71-1

ISBN 13: 978-1-889057-71-2

<u>G+3TiC=C</u>® is a registered trademark.

Nova Press
11659 Mayfield Avenue
Los Angeles, CA USA 90049
1-800-949-6175
info@novapress.net
www.novapress.net

Acknowledgements

Thanks to Gretchen Anderson for doing the narration for the CD. Thanks to Jon Conine at White House Productions, Shelton, Connecticut for recording and editing the CD. Thanks as well to Sybil and Norman Stirling, Patricia Stirling and Graciela Sauro for their comments and suggestions regarding the text. Thanks to Jeff Kolby at *Nova Press* for his support.

Also by Bruce Stirling

Speaking and Writing Strategies for the TOEFL iBT

Available at Amazon.com and as a phone app.
Visit www.argumentmapping.com for more.

Contents

Who is this book for?

Are you studying for the TOEFL test? Do you need to learn academic English vocabulary to increase your TOEFL score? Do you also need to improve your typing skills so you can type your TOEFL essays faster and more accurately on test day? If you said "Yes!" to any of these questions, then this book is for you.

How is this TOEFL book different?

This TOEFL book is different because it uses an integrated vocabulary learning system called recycling. Recycling is simple. Each exercise is divided into four quizzes. Quiz #1, a multiple-choice vocabulary quiz, introduces ten new words. Next, you will do Quiz #2. Quiz #2 is a sentence-completion quiz based on the ten words in Quiz #1. Next, you will do Quiz #3, a spelling quiz. The speaker on the CD will say the same ten words in turn. You will then have ten seconds to spell each word by saying it and typing it. Finally, you will do Quiz #4. Quiz #4 is a 60-word typing test based on the ten new words you have been recycling through Quizzes #1, #2 and #3, plus words, phrases and idioms recycled from previous exercises.

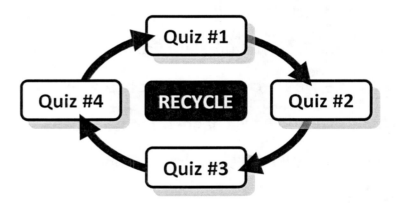

Why Recycling?

Recycling is an effective way to acquire a TOEFL-level vocabulary because you are continually integrating and applying new words across four different contexts (quizzes) using six TOEFL skill sets: reading, listening, speaking, writing, spelling and typing. Recycling will help you remember each new word, phrase and idiom more effectively so you can apply it more proficiently on test day. No other TOEFL text offers such an integrated approach to acquiring a TOEFL-level vocabulary.

Typing: An Essential TOEFL Strategy

To get a high TOEFL score, you must have an academic English vocabulary. You must also be good at typing. Why? Because accurate typing means fewer mistakes. Fewer mistakes means higher essay scores. This text book will teach you essential typing strategies based on the words, phrases and idioms you will recycle across 50 lessons. By doing so, you will increase your typing proficiency and be test ready. This brings us to the next point: How accurately can you type in English? Let's find out.

Diagnostic Typing Test

<u>Directions:</u> √ You have one minute to type the 60-word passage below.

√ Include all punctuation and capital letters.

Topical unity means you focus on one topic from start to finish. If you suddenly introduce a new and unrelated topic, you are changing topics. For example, you are writing about pizza when you suddenly change to TOEFL. This obvious change in topic direction is called a topic digression. This will result in a lack of topical unity and coherence.

Calculating Words-Per-Minute (WPM)

If you made one mistake on the 60-word diagnostic typing test, you can type 59 wpm (60 – 1 = 59 words per minute), two mistakes, 58 wpm, etc.

<u>Note</u>: A letter not capitalized is a mistake. A comma in the wrong place is a mistake. A missing comma is a mistake. Record your wpm score on page 201.

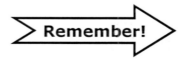

If you type less than 35 wpm, you should learn and practice typing strategies starting on page 172 before you do the recycling exercises.

Recycling Exercises

<u>Directions</u>: √ Each recycling exercise is divided into four quizzes: 1) multiple-choice quiz; 2) sentence-completion quiz; 3) spelling quiz; 4) 60-word typing test. Time yourself when doing each.

√ Do all four quizzes sequentially to maximize the recycling learning process.

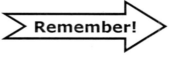

√ When choosing a multiple-choice answer (Quiz #1), do not look for the perfect answer. For TOEFL, and for this text, there are no perfect answers. Choose the multiple-choice answer you think is closest in meaning.

√ Answer all multiple-choice questions even if you do not know the answer. For TOEFL, you will not lose a point if you answer a multiple-choice question incorrectly, so guess and move on.

√ For the sentence-completion quiz (Quiz #2), you will have to use the appropriate part of speech to complete each sentence. For example, you might have to change a singular noun to a plural noun, or a base verb to the infinitive according to the syntax of the sentence.

√ When you have finished all 50 exercises, check your scores on page 201. Recycle those exercises you scored low on.

√ Abbreviations: n = noun, v = verb, adj = adjective, adv = adverb, phr = phrase, id = idiom, conj = conjunction.

EXERCISE 1-A — Multiple-Choice Quiz

Directions: You have 2 minutes to complete this task. Do not use a dictionary. Check your answers on page 192. Record your score on page 201.

1. carnivore (n)

a. plant eater
b. meat eater
c. meat and plant eater
d. primarily a meat eater

2. prey on (v)

a. to look for
b. to think about
c. to hunt
d. to communicate with God

3. accelerate (v)

a. to slow down suddenly
b. to speed up quickly
c. to take one's time
d. to wander

4. camouflage (n)

a. to hide by disguise or protective coloring
b. hunting by hiding
c. a desert animal used for transportation
d. synonym for "color"

5. astounding (adj)

a. amazing
b. incredible
c. unbelievable
d. all of the above

6. resolute (adj)

a. reviled
b. harmonious
c. determined
d. cautious

7. diurnal (adj)

a. active at night
b. active at dawn
c. active at twilight
d. active during the day

8. species (n)

a. organisms capable of breeding and producing offspring of both genders
b. specialized animals living in small groups in Africa
c. large group of animals living in special areas
d. large warm-blooded animals

9. attain (v)

a. to reach
b. to obtain
c. to complete
d. to borrow

10. eschew (v)

a. to chew on
b. to avoid
c. to go after
d. to bargain with

EXERCISE 1-B   Sentence-Completion Quiz

Directions: You have 5 minutes to complete this task. Check your answers on page 192. Record your score on page 201.

Word List	carnivore • prey on • accelerate • camouflage • astounding • resolute • diurnal • species • attain • eschew •

1. Heshu got a perfect 120 on the TOEFL test. That's _____ !

2. Every hour all over the world, three _____ become extinct.

3. Soldiers wear _____ so they will not be seen on the battlefield.

4. Bats are nocturnal. They hunt at night. Deer are crepuscular. They are active at dawn and dusk. Cheetahs are _____ . They hunt during the day.

5. Lions _____ zebras.

6. When a plane takes off, it _____ to reach maximum take off speed.

7. Hernando is very _____ . When he makes up his mind, nothing can change it.

8. The opposite of _____ is herbivore.

9. Sachi studied hard and _____ her goal of becoming a surgeon.

10. Joan _____ peanuts because she is allergic to them.

EXERCISE 1-C — Spelling Quiz – CD Disc #1

Directions: √ Go to track #1 on CD #1.

√ For this quiz, you will hear a word, a phrase or an idiom. You will hear it twice. You will then have ten seconds to type it.

√ As you type the word(s), say each letter.

√ Check your answers in the word list on the previous page.

√ Record your score on page 201.

EXERCISE 1-D — 60-Word Typing Test

Directions: You have 60 seconds to type the following passage. When you are finished, calculate your wpm score. Record your score on page 201.

The cheetah, a species of cat, is found only in Africa. Cheetahs, which are carnivores, are diurnal. They eschew larger animals like zebras and prey on gazelles and impalas instead. The cheetah's spotted fur is excellent camouflage. Quickly accelerating, cheetahs can attain speeds of 120 mph. That is astounding. However, they can only run short distances before they must rest.

WPM Score = / 60

EXERCISE 2-A   Multiple-Choice Quiz

Directions: You have 2 minutes to complete this task. Do not use a dictionary. Check your answers on page 192. Record your score on page 201.

1. proficiency (n)

a. skill and knowledge
b. easy and effortless
c. luck and timing
d. checking and rechecking

2. coherent (adj)

a. clear
b. understandable
c. intelligible
d. all of the above

3. rate (v)

a. to rescind
b. to score
c. to mark up
d. to reason

4. holistic (adj)

a. refers to the hole
b. refers to the whole
c. refers to the pieces
d. refers to the details

5. distractor (n)

a. for TOEFL, a correct answer
b. for TOEFL, no answer
c. for TOEFL, an answer that looks right but is wrong
d. for TOEFL, the perfect answer

6. selective task (phr)

a. constructive task
b. difficult task
c. flexible task
d. multiple-choice task

7. constructive task (phr)

a. selective task
b. development task
c. non-TOEFL task
d. attainable task

8. thesis (n)

a. opinion
b. position
c. claim
d. all of the above

9. integral part of (phr)

a. important part of
b. not an important part of
c. piece of the whole
d. the whole piece

10. intelligible (adj)

a. understandable
b. clear
c. coherent
d. all of the above

EXERCISE 2-B	Sentence-Completion Quiz

Directions: You have 5 minutes to complete this task. Check your answers on page 192. Record your score on page 201.

<u>Word</u> <u>List</u>	proficiency • coherent • rate • holistic • distractor • thesis • selective task • constructive task • integral part of • intelligible •

1. The most important part of your independent essay is your _____ .

2. A _____ TOEFL essay is intelligible.

3. For each TOEFL reading and listening question, you get four answer choices. Two choices are obviously wrong, one is right, and one is a _____ .

4. _____ means skill and knowledge.

5. ETS calls the TOEFL reading and listening questions _____

6. The TOEFL speaking and writing questions are called _____ .

7. Lee's handwriting is so bad it is not _____ .

8. The personal computer is an _____ daily life in the U.S.

9. Traditional Chinese medicine is based on a _____ approach.

10. Your two TOEFL essays will be _____ holistically.

EXERCISE 2-C | Spelling Quiz – Track #2

Directions: √ Go to track #2 on CD #1.

√ For this quiz, you will hear a word, a phrase or an idiom. You will hear it twice. You will then have ten seconds to type it.

√ As you type the word(s), say each letter.

√ Check your answers in the word list on the previous page.

√ Record your score on page 201.

EXERCISE 2-D | 60-Word Typing Test

Directions: You have 60 seconds to type the following passage. When you are finished, calculate your wpm score. Record your score on page 201.

The TOEFL iBT is an English-language proficiency test. It consists of selective and constructive tasks. Reading and listening are selective tasks. Each question includes a distractor. The speaking and writing sections are constructive tasks. A thesis is an integral part of a coherent independent essay. Coherence means your argument is intelligible. Your spoken and written responses will be rated holistically.

WPM Score =   / 60

EXERCISE 3-A   Multiple-Choice Quiz

Directions: You have 2 minutes to complete this task. Do not use a dictionary. Check your answers on page 192. Record your score on page 201.

1. agrarian (adj)

a. related to fields and land and farmers
b. related to oceans and rivers and fishermen
c. related to math and physics and professors
d. related to cars and trucks and mechanics

2. fertile (adj)

a. good for growing
b. rich in nutrients
c. productive
d. all of the above

3. enervating (adj)

a. exciting
b. lazy
c. exhausting
d. afraid

4. reliable (adj)

a. can communicate with
b. can abide with
c. can rely on
d. can lie on

5. prosper (v)

a. to succeed economically
b. to fail romantically
c. to believe resolutely
d. to realize eventually

6. assiduous (adj)

a. lazy
b. smart
c. shy
d. hard working

7. undergo (v)

a. to experience
b. to go through
c. to pass through
d. all of the above

8. transformation (n)

a. process of learning
b. process of changing
c. process of shaming
d. process of taming

9. chaotic (adj)

a. a state of constant change
b. a state of no change
c. a state of equilibrium
d. a state of calm

10. emancipated (adj)

a. enslaved
b. inferior
c. free
d. superior

EXERCISE 3-B   Sentence-Completion Quiz

Directions: You have 5 minutes to complete this task. Check your answers on page 192. Record your score on page 201.

> Word
> List
>
> agrarian • fertile • enervating • reliable • prosper • assiduous •
> undergo • transformation • chaotic • emancipated •

1. When Abraham Lincoln entered Richmond, the defeated capital of the slave-owning south, he was welcomed by _____ slaves.

2. Black soil means the land is very _____ .

3. Checking and rechecking these customer accounts is so _____ .

4. Banaz's life is so _____ . She is always trying to do five things at once.

5. It was a big _____ for Sahiba when she moved to Canada and married David.

6. An _____ worker is a resolute worker.

7. When you move to a new country, you _____ many changes, such as learning how to speak a new language.

8. Why do I need a new car? My old car is perfectly _____ .

9. Beata's new hat company has really begun to _____ .

10. In North America, many Native Americans followed the buffalo for food while others lived in villages. These Native Americans grew corn thus they were _____ while the hunters were nomadic.

EXERCISE 3-C	Spelling Quiz – Track #3

Directions: √ Go to track #3 on CD #1.

√ For this quiz, you will hear a word, a phrase or an idiom. You will hear it twice. You will then have ten seconds to type it.

√ As you type the word(s), say each letter.

√ Check your answers in the word list on the previous page.

√ Record your score on page 201.

EXERCISE 3-D	60-Word Typing Test

Directions: You have 60 seconds to type the following passage. When you are finished, calculate your wpm score. Record your score on page 201.

One day, Zachary Zilgenz underwent a transformation. He gave up a chaotic big city life and moved to a fertile valley where he felt emancipated living an agrarian life. He bought a reliable tractor and worked the land assiduously. Yet, just as he began to prosper, Zachary underwent another transformation. He realized that the agrarian life can be very enervating.

WPM Score = _____ / 60

EXERCISE 4-A   Multiple-Choice Quiz

Directions: You have 2 minutes to complete this task. Do not use a dictionary. Check your answers on page 192. Record your score on page 201.

1. envisage (v)

a. to calculate
b. to visualize
c. to actualize
d. to summarize

2. innovate (v)

a. to develop or create something new
b. to introduce and teach something old
c. to produce and sell something expensive
d. to consider and evaluate your options

3. merge (v)

a. to separate
b. to measure
c. to mend
d. to unite

4. trailblazer (n)

a. leader
b. pioneer
c. pathfinder
d. all of the above

5. wary (adj)

a. wonderful
b. war-like
c. intelligent
d. watchful

6. versatile (adj)

a. can be used very often
b. can be used only two ways
c. can not be used at all
d. can be used many ways

7. inasmuch as (conj)

a. because
b. since
c. owing to the fact that
d. all of the above

8. vulnerable (adj)

a. open to attack
b. closed to attack
c. ready to attack
d. capable of attack

9. germinate (v)

a. to start to emancipate
b. to start to feed
c. to start to learn
d. to start to grow

10. fundamental (adj)

a. basic
b. essential
c. central part of
d. all of the above

EXERCISE 4-B   Sentence-Completion Quiz

<u>Directions</u>: You have 5 minutes to complete this task. Check your answers on page 192. Record your score on page 201.

<u>Word</u>   envisage • innovate • merge • trailblazer • wary • vulnerable •
<u>List</u>   versatile • inasmuch as • germinate • fundamental •

1. Sandra Day O'Connor was a _____ . She was the first women elected to the United States Supreme Court.

2. Old technologies always _____ with new technologies. For example, radio _____ with television. Now television is _____ with personal computers.

3. Water is a _____ human requirement.

4. Apple is one of the most _____ companies in the world. They are always introducing cutting-edge products.

5. Hiro needs a high TOEFL score _____ he wants to go to Harvard.

6. When the Pilgrims landed in America, they _____ a new home for themselves in a new land.

7. Wild animals are very _____ . They have to be in order to survive.

8. The seed has _____ . Next, it will grow into a beautiful flower.

9. If you do not wear a seat belt, you are _____ to serious injury.

10. Naheed is really _____ . She can play soccer, tennis, baseball, and ping pong.

EXERCISE 4-C — Spelling Quiz – Track #4

Directions: √ Go to track #4 on CD #1.

√ For this quiz, you will hear a word, a phrase or an idiom. You will hear it twice. You will then have ten seconds to type it.

√ As you type the word(s), say each letter.

√ Check your answers in the word list on the previous page.

√ Record your score on page 201.

EXERCISE 4-D — 60-Word Typing Test

Directions: You have 60 seconds to type the following passage. When you are finished, calculate your wpm score. Record your score on page 201.

> The internet is so versatile. It is a fundamental part of daily life in the United States. The idea germinated at M.I.T. and Stanford. Bill Gates is also a trailblazing innovator. But even his fertile mind couldn't envisage how the internet would merge science and art. Yet some are still wary inasmuch as personal computers are vulnerable to internet viruses.

WPM Score =   / 60

EXERCISE 5-A | Multiple-Choice Quiz

Directions: You have 2 minutes to complete this task. Do not use a dictionary. Check your answers on page 192. Record your score on page 201.

1. a myriad of (phr)

a. lots
b. abundant
c. great number
d. all of the above

2. a plethora of (phr)

a. excessive
b. far too much or many
c. more than is practical or useful
d. all of the above

3. allude to (v)

a. to ask casually
b. to refer to casually
c. to refer to formally
d. to refuse always

4. analogous (adj)

a. related to
b. connected to
c. comparable to
d. all of the above

5. abundance (n)

a. more than enough
b. plenty
c. full of
d. all of the above

6. connote (v)

a. to give meaning beyond the literal definition
b. to give added expression in conversation
c. to give a wise answer to a tough question
d. to suggest or imply that something is wrong

7. domestic (adj)

a. referring to life around the house
b. referring to life in the corporate world
c. referring to life in college
d. referring to life in the entertainment world

8. dissimilar (adj)

a. almost the same
b. not similar
c. rarely the same
d. always similar

9. indeed (adv)

a. without a doubt
b. in fact
c. certainly
d. all of the above

10. quite (adv)

a. very
b. exactly
c. really
d. all of the above

EXERCISE 5-B   Sentence-Completion Quiz

Directions: You have 5 minutes to complete this task. Check your answers on page 192. Record your score on page 201.

Word List	a myriad of • a plethora of • allude to • analogous • quite • abundance • connote • domestic • dissimilar • indeed •

1. TOEFL, IELTS, and TOEIC have _____ testing methods.

2. There is definitely not an _____ of water in the Sahara.

3. The name Nelson Mandela _____ greatness and resolution.

4. Tigers in India are wild or "feral" whereas house cats in America are _____ .

5. The personal computer is an integral part of daily life, _____ .

6. Are Coke and Pepsi really that _____ ?

7. Joe has _____ money problems inasmuch as he has been unable to find a job.

8. At university, you have _____ courses from which you can choose your major.

9. These new shoes don't fit _____ right.

10. Whenever the president gives a speech, he always _____ his wife and how she has been the biggest influence in his life.

EXERCISE 5-C | Spelling Quiz – Track #5

<u>Directions</u>: √ Go to track #5 on CD #1.

√ For this quiz, you will hear a word, a phrase or an idiom. You will hear it twice. You will then have ten seconds to type it.

√ As you type the word(s), say each letter.

√ Check your answers in the word list on the previous page.

√ Record your score on page 201.

EXERCISE 5-D | 60-Word Typing Test

<u>Directions</u>: You have 60 seconds to type the following passage. When you are finished, calculate your wpm score. Record your score on page 201.

Indeed, "a myriad of" might seem analogous to "a plethora of." However, these two phrases are quite dissimilar. If you have a myriad of chores, for example, you're alluding to the fact that you have an abundance of domestic responsibilities. In other words, you have lots of housework to do whereas a plethora of chores connotes too much enervating housework.

WPM Score =   / 60

Review# 1

Directions: You have 60 seconds to complete this task. Do not use a dictionary. Check your answers on page 192. Record your score on page 201.

1. distractor (n)

a. for TOEFL, a correct answer
b. for TOEFL, no answer
c. for TOEFL, an answer that looks right but is wrong
d. for TOEFL, the only answer

2. species (n)

a. organisms capable of breeding and producing offspring of both genders
b. specialized animals living in small groups in Africa
c. large group of animals living in special areas
d. large warm blooded animals

3. eschew (v)

a. to chew on
b. to avoid
c. to go after
d. to bargain with

4. emancipated (adj)

a. enslaved
b. inferior
c. free
d. superior

5. inasmuch as (conj)

a. because
b. since
c. owing to the fact that
d. all of the above

6. a myriad of (adj)

a. lots
b. abundant
c. great number
d. all of the above

7. quite (adv)

a. very
b. exactly
c. really
d. all of the above

8. versatile (adj)

a. can be used very often
b. can be used only two ways
c. can not be used at all
d. can be used many ways

9. agrarian (adj)

a. related to fields and land and farmers
b. related to oceans and rivers and fishermen
c. related to math and physics and professors
d. related to cars and trucks and mechanics

10. thesis (n)

a. opinion
b. position
c. claim
d. all of the above

EXERCISE 6-A | Multiple-Choice Quiz

<u>Directions</u>: You have 2 minutes to complete this task. Do not use a dictionary. Check your answers on page 192. Record your score on page 201.

1. harbinger (n)

a. sign
b. passenger
c. harbor
d. all of the above

2. perch (v)

a. to leave a comfortable place
b. to search and find a nice place
c. to provide shelter in a safe place
d. to rest or settle in a high place

3. offspring (n)

a. parents
b. uncles
c. grandparents
d. children

4. precarious (adj)

a. dangerous
b. doubtful
c. not secure
d. all of the above

5. quest (n)

a. to seek
b. to look for
c. to search
d. all of the above

6. profuse (adj)

a. not many
b. an average number
c. great abundance
d. correct amount

7. infer (v)

a. to conclude from facts
b. to research the facts
c. to describe important facts
d. to require legal facts

8. thaw (v)

a. to change from ice to water
b. to melt
c. to warm up
d. all of the above

9. keen (adj)

a. very clean
b. very warm
c. very dull
d. very sensitive

10. brood (n)

a. group of old animals
b. young children of one family
c. cousins
d. first queen

EXERCISE 6-B | Sentence-Completion Quiz

Directions: You have 5 minutes to complete this task. Check your answers on page 192. Record your score on page 201.

Word List	harbinger • perch • offspring • precarious • quest • profuse • to infer • thaw • keen • brood •

1. In the late 1980s, relations between the Soviet Union and the U.S. began to _____ .

2. Dogs have a _____ sense of smell.

3. When the leaves fall in autumn, it is a _____ of winter.

4. Eagles _____ at the top of the highest trees.

5. When Bess secretly saw Sam offer Daisy a diamond ring, she _____ that Sam had just proposed to Daisy.

6. Rabbits produce many _____ .

7. That rope bridge might look _____ , but it is really quite strong.

8. King Arthur and his knights were on a _____ to find the Holy Grail.

9. The mother bear moved her _____ across the river.

10. After winning an Oscar, the actor gave _____ thanks to everyone.

EXERCISE 6-C   Spelling Quiz – Track #6

Directions: √ Go to track #6 on CD #1.

√ For this quiz, you will hear a word, a phrase or an idiom. You will hear it twice. You will then have ten seconds to type it.

√ As you type the word(s), say each letter.

√ Check your answers in the word list on the previous page.

√ Record your score on page 201.

EXERCISE 6-D   60-Word Typing Test

Directions: You have 60 seconds to type the following passage. When you are finished, calculate your wpm score. Record your score on page 201.

Robins are a harbinger of spring. When you see one perching on a branch, or searching for food, you can infer that winter's over. Robins arrive in profuse numbers after the first thaw. Their offspring are born in nests built in precarious places. With keen eyes, the parent birds are resolute in their daily quest for food for their brood.

WPM Score =   / 60

EXERCISE 7-A   Multiple-Choice Quiz

Directions: You have 2 minutes to complete this task. Do not use a dictionary. Check your answers on page 192. Record your score on page 201.

1. impecunious (adj)

a. always sad
b. always poor
c. always happy
d. always rich

2. benevolent (adj)

a. generous
b. kind
c. good
d. all of the above

3. inveterate (adj)

a. new habit
b. changing habit
c. uncommon habit
d. established habit

4. reimburse (v)

a. to delay paying
b. to avoid paying
c. to pay back
d. to pay only half

5. subsist on (v)

a. to live on
b. to lie on
c. to rely on
d. to inform on

6. quite the contrary (phr)

a. in conclusion
b. in addition
c. the exact opposite
d. finally

7. all in all (phr)

a. when everything is considered
b. in the final analysis
c. when all is said and done
d. all of the above

8. judicious (adj)

a. demonstrating bad judgment
b. demonstrating no judgment
c. demonstrating good judgment
d. demonstrating before a judge

9. insinuate (v)

a. to suggest
b. to request
c. to insulate
d. to investigate

10. suffice it to say (phr)

a.   in short
b.   it is enough to say
c.   no more is needed to add
d.   all of the above

EXERCISE 7-B　　Sentence-Completion Quiz

<u>Directions</u>: You have 5 minutes to complete this task. Check your answers on page 192. Record your score on page 201.

<u>Word</u> <u>List</u>	impecunious • benevolent • inveterate • reimburse • all in all • subsist on • quite the contrary • judicious • insinuate • suffice it to say •

1. Ricardo thinks that global warming is nothing to worry about. Sam, _____ , believes that global warming is a serious problem.

2. Rita is quite prosperous; however, when she was a student she was _____ .

3. _____ , the party was a great success.

4. Man cannot _____ water alone.

5. When are the banks going _____ the government for all the money they borrowed after the stock market crashed?

6. _____ , we could all use a vacation.

7. The _____ queen works assiduously to help her people prosper.

8. Mikael is an _____ gambler. He will bet on anything.

9. The professor _____ that Herman should study harder.

10. Surjit is always very _____ with her money. She never makes a big purchase without first doing a complete price comparison.

EXERCISE 7-C   Spelling Quiz – Track #7

Directions: √ Go to track #7 on CD #1.

√ For this quiz, you will hear a word, a phrase or an idiom. You will hear it twice. You will then have ten seconds to type it.

√ As you type the word(s), say each letter.

√ Check your answers in the word list on the previous page.

√ Record your score on page 201.

EXERCISE 7-D   60-Word Typing Test

Directions: You have 60 seconds to type the following passage. When you are finished, calculate your wpm score. Record your score on page 201.

Suffice it to say, Frank's inveterate spending has left him in an impecunious state. Consequently, he is feeling quite low. Lately, he's been subsisting on loans from benevolent friends he has yet to reimburse. I don't mean to insinuate that Frank is a bad man, quite the contrary. I just wish he were more judicious with his use of money.

WPM Score =   / 60

EXERCISE 8-A — Multiple-Choice Quiz

Directions: You have 2 minutes to complete this task. Do not use a dictionary. Check your answers on page 192. Record your score on page 201.

1. posthumously (adv)

a. after death
b. when born
c. as an adult
d. in old age

2. hue (n)

a. color
b. sound
c. vision
d. prayer

3. masterpiece (n)

a. average work
b. great work
c. ancient work
d. latest work

4. saturated (adj)

a. drenched
b. soaked
c. full of
d. all of the above

5. towering (adj)

a. lower than the rest
b. equal to everyone
c. worst of the worst
d. best of the best

6. snub (v)

a. to ignore
b. to avoid
c. to shun
d. all of the above

7. mercurial (adj)

a. changing predictably
b. changing unpredictably
c. made of mercury
d. planet

8. palette (n)

a. artist's brush keeping box
b. artist's paint mixing board
c. artist's frame box
d. artist's planning board

9. shimmer (v)

a. to flicker like sunlight
b. to shine like sunlight
c. to move like sunlight
d. all of the above

10. unerring (adj)

a. always making a mistake
b. rarely making a mistake
c. never making a mistake
d. eventually making a mistake

EXERCISE 8-B   Sentence-Completion Quiz

Directions: You have 5 minutes to complete this task. Check your answers on page 192. Record your score on page 201.

Word List	posthumously • hue • masterpiece • saturated • towering • snub • mercurial • palette • shimmer • unerring •

1. Michael Jackson is as famous _____ as he was alive.

2. Traditionally, an artist's _____ is a board used for mixing paints.

3. Steve Jobs, founder of Apple Computer, created the first consumer PC, music for the web using iTunes, the iPod, and the iPhone. Suffice it to say, he has an _____ genius for innovation and marketing.

4. James Joyce is a _____ literary figure in the west.

5. When the sun sets, Jan likes to sit and watch the sunlight _____ on the lake.

6. When Phil asked the movie star for her autograph, she _____ him.

7. A _____ temper is often a harbinger of trouble.

8. Van Gogh used a myriad of _____ .

9. It has rained so much, the ground is now _____ with water.

10. Indeed, the opera *Carmen* by Georges Bizet is a _____ .

EXERCISE 8-C   Spelling Quiz – Track #8

Directions: √ Go to track #8 on CD #1.

√ For this quiz, you will hear a word, a phrase or an idiom. You will hear it twice. You will then have ten seconds to type it.

√ As you type the word(s), say each letter.

√ Check your answers in the word list on the previous page.

√ Record your score on page 201.

EXERCISE 8-D   60-Word Typing Test

Directions: You have 60 seconds to type the following passage. When you are finished, calculate your wpm score. Record your score on page 201.

Van Gogh is a towering figure in the art world. The hues of his early work are quite dark while the colors of his later work are so saturated with light they seem to shimmer. Van Gogh had an unerring palette and a mercurial temper. For that the art world snubbed him. Only posthumously were his masterpieces and genius recognized.

WPM Score =   / 60

EXERCISE 9-A   Multiple-Choice Quiz

Directions: You have 2 minutes to complete this task. Do not use a dictionary. Check your answers on page 192. Record your score on page 201.

1. ology (suffix)

a. meaning the study of
b. meaning the center of
c. meaning the father of
d. meaning the mother of

2. geology (n)

a. the study of water
b. the study of rocks
c. the study of stars
d. the study of mathematics

3. sociology (n)

a. the study of sport
b. the study of rocks
c. the study of society
d. the study of diseases

4. archeology (n)

a. the study of new cultures
b. the study of art and music
c. the study of medicine
d. the study of historic or prehistoric cultures

5. criminology (n)

a. the study of crime and criminals
b. the study of time and crime
c. the study of fish and animals
d. the study of old words

6. psychology (n)

a. study of time and society
b. study of blood and race
c. study of the mind and behavior
d. all of the above

7. climatology (n)

a. the study of climates
b. the study of water
c. the study of cats
d. the study of climbing

8. anthropology (n)

a. the study of the mind
b. the study of music
c. the study of humans
d. the study of shells

9. meteorology (n)

a. the study of meteors
b. the study of the weather
c. the study of the poles
d. the study of rocks

10. discombobulated (adj)

a. confused
b. uncertain
c. not clear
d. all of the above

EXERCISE 9-B	Sentence-Completion Quiz

Directions: You have 5 minutes to complete this task. Check your answers on page 192. Record your score on page 201.

Word
List

ology • geology • sociology • archeology • criminology • psychology • climatology • anthropology • meteorology • discombobulated •

1. _____ was Sherlock Holmes' specialty.

2. Indiana Jones has a passion for _____ .

3. _____ helps us understand global warming.

4. People who study the weather are experts in _____ .

5. Is _____ a prefix or a suffix?

6. If you want to learn about rocks and how the earth was made, you should study _____ .

7. The independent essay prompt really _____ Tomoko.

8. Amina is a scientist who studies how the mind affects behavior. Her field is called _____ .

9. _____ teaches us how cultural forces affect the family structure.

10. Louise wants to study social customs and how they have influenced the development of cultures world wide. Her friend suggested that she study _____ at university.

EXERCISE 9-C Spelling Quiz – Track #9

Directions: √ Go to track #9 on CD #1.

√ For this quiz, you will hear a word, a phrase or an idiom. You will hear it twice. You will then have ten seconds to type it.

√ As you type the word(s), say each letter.

√ Check your answers in the word list on the previous page.

√ Record your score on page 201.

EXERCISE 9-D 60-Word Typing Test

Directions: You have 60 seconds to type the following passage. When you are finished, calculate your wpm score. Record your score on page 201.

Geology, sociology, meteorology, archeology, criminology, psychology, climatology and anthropology. Those are just a few English words that end with the suffix ology. Ology comes from the Greek word logos. Logos means "the study of." Many words are formed using ology, such as physiology, vulcanology, apiology, cosmetology, biology, astrology, hydrology and musicology. Are you feeling a little discombobulated? How about TOEFLology?

WPM Score =   / 60

EXERCISE 10-A | Sentence-Completion Quiz

Directions: You have 2 minutes to complete this task. Do not use a dictionary. Check your answers on page 192. Record your score on page 201.

1. dwelling (n)

a. home
b. place to live
c. abode
d. all of the above

2. inhabit (v)

a. to live outside of
b. to live in front of
c. to live without
d. to live in

3. opulent (adj)

a. demonstrating great wealth
b. demonstrating a bad choice
c. demonstrating no wealth
d. demonstrating a good choice

4. Spartan (adj)

a. simple
b. basic
c. frugal
d. all of the above

5. renounce (v)

a. to throw up
b. to show up
c. to drink up
d. to give up

6. per capita (phr)

a. per person
b. equal for some
c. income tax
d. foreign investments

7. void of (phr)

a. full of
b. empty of
c. half full of
d. in need of

8. contrivances (n)

a. mechanical things
b. fundamental domestic things
c. electrical things
d. all of the above

9. novel (adj)

a. old
b. young
c. new
d. ancient

10. environs (n)

a. environment
b. place
c. area
d. all of the above

EXERCISE 10-B Word-Insertion Quiz

Directions: You have 5 minutes to complete this task. Check your answers on page 192. Record your score on page 201.

Word List	dwelling • inhabit • opulent • Spartan • renounce • void of • per capita • contrivances • novel • environs •

1. Pamela's kitchen is full of the latest _____ .

2. The iPod is quite a _____ idea.

3. Some _____ houses are really quite astounding.

4. I would avoid X Street and the surrounding _____ late at night.

5. What is the _____ income of your country?

6. Anthropologists tell us that early agrarians led _____ lives.

7. In winter, Eskimos live in _____ made of snow and ice called igloos.

8. Because the Sahara is _____ water, few people can survive there. Those who do are nomads traveling between water sources.

9. Cheetahs _____ the arid plains of Africa.

10. Marcus has _____ coffee however he has yet to _____ smoking.

EXERCISE 10-C   Spelling Quiz – Track #10

Directions: √ Go to track #10 on CD #1.

√ For this quiz, you will hear a word, a phrase or an idiom. You will hear it twice. You will then have ten seconds to type it.

√ As you type the word(s), say each letter.

√ Check your answers in the word list on the previous page.

√ Record your score on page 201.

EXERCISE 10-D   60-Word Typing Test

Directions: You have 60 seconds to type the following passage. When you are finished, calculate your wpm score. Record your score on page 201.

What kind of dwelling do you inhabit? If you live in an opulent house, then the per capita income of your neighborhood is probably quite high. Many, however, have renounced opulence for more Spartan environs void of all the novel contrivances that come with luxury living. These individuals often buy secondhand furniture and fix it up in order to save money.

WPM Score =   / 60

Review #2

Directions: You have 60 seconds to complete this task. Do not use a dictionary. Check your answers on page 192. Record your score on page 201.

1. archeology (n)

a. the study of new cultures
b. the study of art and music
c. the study of medicine
d. the study of historic or prehistoric cultures

2. all in all (phr)

a. when everything is considered
b. in the final analysis
c. when all is said and done
d. all of the above

3. posthumously (adv)

a. after death
b. when born
c. as an adult
d. in old age

4. harbinger (n)

a. sign
b. passenger
c. harbor
d. all of the above

5. per capita (phr)

a. per person
b. equal for some
c. income tax
d. foreign investments

6. infer (v)

a. to conclude from facts
b. to research the facts
c. to describe important facts
d. to require legal facts

7. suffice it to say (phr)

a. in short
b. it is enough to say
c. no more is needed to add
d. all of the above

8. hue (n)

a. color
b. sound
c. vision
d. prayer

9. ology (suffix)

a. means the study of
b. means the center of
c. means the father of
d. means the mother of

10. inhabit (v)

a. to live outside of
b. to live in front of
c. to live without
d. to live in

EXERCISE 11-A   Multiple-Choice Quiz

Directions: You have 2 minutes to complete this task. Do not use a dictionary. Check your answers on page 192. Record your score on page 201.

1. precipitation (n)

a. rain
b. snow
c. hail
d. all of the above

2. drought (n)

a. long period of no precipitation
b. long period of war
c. long period of peace
d. long period of creation

3. famine (n)

a. extreme lack of food
b. extreme lack of rain
c. extreme lack of land
d. extreme lack of work

4. omen (n)

a. sign
b. king
c. God
d. story

5. render (v)

a. to change
b. to transform
c. to alter
d. all of the above

6. arable (adj)

a. bad for farming
b. good for building on
c. good for farming
d. sold for farming

7. arid (adj)

a. lacking moisture
b. no water
c. dry
d. all of the above

8. abandon (v)

a. to return to often
b. to give up and leave
c. to abide by always
d. to transform quickly

9. downfall (n)

a. sudden loss of knowledge
b. sudden loss of wealth and power
c. sudden plethora of problems
d. sudden abundance

10. destitute (adj)

a. lacking nothing
b. lacking everything
c. lacking time
d. all of the above

EXERCISE 11-B   Sentence-Completion Quiz

Directions: You have 5 minutes to complete this task. Check your answers on page 192. Record your score on page 201.

> | Word List | drought • famine • precipitation • omen • render • arable • arid • abandon • downfall • destitute • |
> |---|---|

1. The _____ has lasted more than five years. Even now there is no rain.

2. The homeless man on the corner is obviously _____ for a myriad of reasons.

3. _____ can be any form of water that falls from the sky, for example snow, rain, sleet or hail.

4. Long ago, a king's position was always precarious. His _____ could happen at any time.

5. From an _____ , agrarian people could infer many things, such as a year of rain or a year of drought.

6. A dead battery will _____ a cell phone unusable.

7. Petra had to _____ the idea of completing her university degree in two years instead of four.

8. "Feast or _____ " is a common expression analogous to "Times are either really good or really bad with no in between."

9. Some believe that _____ land is more valuable than gold.

10. Arizona is quite _____ .

EXERCISE 11-C	Spelling Quiz – Track #11

Directions: √ Go to track #11 on CD #1.

√ For this quiz, you will hear a word, a phrase or an idiom. You will hear it twice. You will then have ten seconds to type it.

√ As you type the word(s), say each letter.

√ Check your answers in the word list on the previous page.

√ Record your score on page 201.

EXERCISE 11-D	60-Word Typing Test

Directions: You have 60 seconds to type the following passage. When you are finished, calculate your wpm score. Record your score on page 201.

A drought means a long period of no precipitation. Because there is no precipitation, the soil becomes arid. Consequently, once fertile land is rendered unarable. This, in turn, leads to famine. Drought has caused the downfall of many civilizations. People had to abandon the land inasmuch as they were left destitute. Many believed that droughts were omens from the Gods.

WPM Score =   **/ 60**

EXERCISE 12-A   Multiple-Choice Quiz

Directions: You have 2 minutes to complete this task. Do not use a dictionary. Check your answers on page 192. Record your score on page 201.

1. notorious (adj)

a. famous for good behavior
b. famous for wise behavior
c. famous for bad behavior
d. famous for judicious behavior

2. nefarious (adj)

a. evil
b. very bad
c. wicked
d. all of the above

3. pervade (v)

a. to leave all parts
b. to introduce all parts
c. to enter all parts
d. to consider all parts

4. ruthless (adj)

a. no fun
b. no mercy
c. no memory
d. no idea

5. reign (v)

a. to rule like a queen or king
b. to control for a time period
c. to exercise authority
d. all of the above

6. unquenchable (adj)

a. always thirsty
b. unable to satisfy
c. always desiring more
d. all of the above

7. repeal (v)

a. to seek justice
b. to rescind officially
c. to make a deal
d. to repeat a deal

8. turbulent (adj)

a. chaotic
b. pacific
c. arid
d. impecunious

9. widespread (adj)

a. happening over a small area
b. happening at the same time
c. happening over a wide area
d. happening once in a while

10. corruption (n)

a.   process of decay
b.   immoral behavior
c.   gain by breaking the law
d.   all of the above

EXERCISE 12-B | Sentence-Completion Quiz

Directions: You have 5 minutes to complete this task. Check your answers on page 192. Record your score on page 201.

Word List	notorious • nefarious • pervade • ruthless • reign • repeal • unquenchable • turbulent • widespread • corruption •

1. Famine in Africa is _____ .

2. The period following the downfall of a monarch or some other political leader is always _____ .

3. Many in America want the government _____ the marijuana laws.

4. Carlos has an _____ desire for perilous sports.

5. Elizabeth the First of England _____ from 1558 to 1603.

6. Is it possible to eliminate government _____ ?

7. Madonna's _____ behavior helped make her famous.

8. Dictators must be _____ in order to survive.

9. James Bond always fights _____ characters.

10. Pollution, particularly in the form of plastic bottles, has _____ all corners of the planet.

EXERCISE 12-C | Spelling Quiz – Track #12

Directions: √ Go to track #12 on CD #1.

√ For this quiz, you will hear a word, a phrase or an idiom. You will hear it twice. You will then have ten seconds to type it.

√ As you type the word(s), say each letter.

√ Check your answers in the word list on the previous page.

√ Record your score on page 201.

EXERCISE 12-D | 60-Word Typing Test

Directions: You have 60 seconds to type the following passage. When you are finished, calculate your wpm score. Record your score on page 201.

The 1920s were turbulent times in America. Chicago is a good example of the chaos. The notorious Al Capone and his nefarious associates saturated the inhabitants of Chicago with illegal alcohol. Capone ruthlessly eliminated other gangs and reigned supreme over widespread corruption that pervaded even the police force. Chicago's unquenchable thirst for alcohol lasted until Prohibition was repealed in 1933.

WPM Score = / 60

EXERCISE 13-A Multiple-Choice Quiz

Directions: You have 2 minutes to complete this task. Do not use a dictionary. Check your answers on page 192. Record your score on page 201.

1. disaster (n)

a. event that results in human loss
b. event that results in financial loss
c. event that results in the loss of part the environment
d. all of the above

2. avalanche (n)

a. snow and ice racing down a mountain
b. snow and ice getting deeper
c. snow and ice melting quickly
d. snow and ice advancing

3. tsunami (n)

a. ocean waves caused by a ship
b. ocean wave caused by an earthquake
c. excellent surfing wave caused by a big storm
d. series of high ocean waves

4. hurricane (n)

a. violent ocean storm
b. tropical cyclonic storm
c. storm with high winds
d. all of the above

5. tornado (n)

a. violent storm
b. cyclonic land storm
c. storm with high winds
d. all of the above

6. placid (adj)

a. mad and upset
b. calm and gentle
c. excited and restless
d. perilous and evil

7. landscape (n)

a. the shape of the land
b. the land in front of the viewer
c. the natural surroundings
d. all of the above

8. deadliest (adj)

a. most friendly
b. most costly
c. most deadly
d. most impecunious

9. sweep through (v)

a. to move through slowly
b. to move through quickly
c. to move through randomly
d. to move through daily

10. shatter (v)

a. to break in many pieces
b. to shift around in a circle
c. to collect many pieces
d. to gather many pieces

EXERCISE 13-B   Sentence-Completion Quiz

Directions: You have 5 minutes to complete this task. Check your answers on page 192. Record your score on page 201.

<u>Word</u> <u>List</u>	disaster • avalanche • tsunami • hurricane • tornado • placid • landscape • deadliest • sweep through • shatter •

1. In Connecticut in the fall, the _____ changes from summer green to a myriad of autumn hues.

2. Every Saturday morning, Fernanda _____ the mall looking for sales.

3. The clown fish is not one of the _____ fishes in the world.

4. Don't drop that crystal glass or it will _____ .

5. _____ claim the lives of many skiers every year.

6. Is it possible to surf a _____ ?

7. An earthquake that kills many people and results in extreme financial loss is an example of a natural _____ .

8. The state of Kansas is notorious for having a lot of _____ .

9. Look at the sunlight shimmering on the _____ lake.

10. When meteorologists name a _____ , they do not use the letters Q, U, X, Y, or Z because few names begin with those letters.

EXERCISE 13-C   Spelling Quiz – Track #13

<u>Directions:</u> √ Go to track #13 on CD #1.

√ For this quiz, you will hear a word, a phrase or an idiom. You will hear it twice. You will then have ten seconds to type it.

√ As you type the word(s), say each letter.

√ Check your answers in the word list on the previous page.

√ Record your score on page 201.

EXERCISE 13-D   60-Word Typing Test

<u>Directions:</u> You have 60 seconds to type the following passage. When you are finished, calculate your wpm score. Record your score on page 201.

Worldwide, natural disasters come in all shapes and sizes, such as tornados, hurricanes, avalanches, and tsunamis. Each can transform a perfectly placid landscape into shattered worlds of profuse suffering. A good example is Hurricane Katrina. Katrina swept through New Orleans in 2005 and killed 1,836 people. Meteorologists say Hurricane Katrina was one of the five deadliest hurricanes in American history.

WPM Score =   / 60

EXERCISE 14-A   Multiple-Choice Quiz

Directions: You have 2 minutes to complete this task. Do not use a dictionary. Check your answers on page 192. Record your score on page 201.

1. profit (v)

a. to benefit from
b. to gain from
c. to make income after all expenses
d. all of the above

2. go bankrupt (v)

a. to be able to pay one's bills
b. to be judged unable to pay one's bills
c. to forget a plethora of unpaid bills
d. to be free to pay no bills

3. take over (v)

a. to take a chance
b. to take control of
c. to take a loss
d. to lose control

4. aggregate (n)

a. big pieces broken into smaller pieces
b. many big and small pieces
c. too many broken pieces
d. small pieces joined to make a big piece

5. acquire (v)

a. to take possession of
b. to own
c. to take control of
d. all of the above

6. share (n)

a. paper signifying a percentage of ownership in a public company
b. a piece of something
c. part of a whole
d. all of the above

7. turn around (v)

a. to go in the same direction
b. to go in the wrong direction
c. to go in a myriad of directions
d. to go in a new direction

8. turn a profit (v)

a. to make money
b. to make a profit
c. to succeed
d. all of the above

9. conglomerate (n)

a. company with many foreign partners
b. company with little or no profit
c. company with only one product
d. company with many large sub divisions of different industries

10. target market (n)

a. particular customers for a particular product
b. market that is profitable
c. market that is transforming
d. a foreign market that is failing

EXERCISE 14-B Sentence-Completion Quiz

<u>Directions</u>: You have 5 minutes to complete this task. Check your answers on page 192. Record your score on page 201.

<u>Word</u> <u>List</u>	profit • go bankrupt • take over • aggregate • acquire • share • turn around • turn a profit • conglomerate • target market •

1. The goal of each company is to _____ .

2. Hollywood's _____ is young American males and foreigners.

3. Concrete, invented by the Romans, is an _____ of mortar, rocks, pieces of ceramic tile, sea shells, and demolished old buildings.

4. Ann and David are hoping _____ some land in the country.

5. Kereshmeh bought one thousand Microsoft _____ and two thousand Apple _____ .

6. Irena is not doing well at school. I hope she can _____ it _____ soon.

7. Looking back, Brad believes he has really _____ from getting his MBA.

8. General Electric (GE), a famous American _____ , was started by Thomas Edison in 1892.

9. Many companies _____ because they do not have a coherent business plan.

10. Napoleon tried to _____ Russia. However, a cold, hard winter rendered his invasion plans useless. Consequently, he retreated in defeat.

EXERCISE 14-C   Spelling Quiz – Track #14

Directions: √ Go to track #14 on CD #1.

√ For this quiz, you will hear a word, a phrase or an idiom. You will hear it twice. You will then have ten seconds to type it.

√ As you type the word(s), say each letter.

√ Check your answers in the word list on the previous page.

√ Record your score on page 201.

EXERCISE 14-D   60-Word Typing Test

Directions: You have 60 seconds to type the following passage. When you are finished, calculate your wpm score. Record your score on page 201.

OUi corporation, a French conglomerate, recently went bankrupt. OUi is an aggregate of financial, aerospace, medical, and energy businesses, none of which has turned a profit in ten years. OUi has tried to turn around, but has failed to acquire a significant share of their target markets. BNZ, a prosperous German company, plans to take over OUi and transform it.

WPM Score =   / 60

EXERCISE 15-A | Multiple-Choice Quiz

Directions: You have 2 minutes to complete this task. Do not use a dictionary. Check your answers on page 192. Record your score on page 201.

1. DNA (n)

a. deoxyribonucleic acid
b. the building blocks of life
c. genetic instructions
d. all of the above

2. quadruped (n)

a. two limb movement
b. eight limb movement
c. movement using no limbs
d. movement using four limbs

3. primate (n)

a. mammals in the order of Primates, including humans and apes
b. mammals in the order of Primates, including only apes
c. gorillas and chimpanzees
d. mammals in the order of Primates, including humans, dogs and cats

4. primarily (adv)

a. mainly
b. usually
c. predominantly
d. all of the above

5. extinct (adj)

a. species still living
b. species becoming fewer
c. species no longer living
d. species struggling to survive

6. endangered (adj)

a. threatened with extinction
b. threatened by man
c. threatened by drought or famine
d. all of the above

7. habitat (n)

a. animal's environment
b. animal's natural home
c. place a species is likely to be seen
d. all of the above

8. herbivore (n)

a. eats only plants
b. eats plants and meat
c. eats only spices
d. eats only meat

9. vanish (v)

a. to envisage
b. to disappear
c. to vanquish
d. to escape

10. irreplaceable (adj)

a. cannot replace
b. cannot substitute
c. impossible to find another
d. all of the above

EXERCISE 15-B   Sentence-Completion Quiz

Directions: You have 5 minutes to complete this task. Check your answers on page 192. Record your score on page 201.

Word List	DNA • quadruped • primate • primarily • extinct • endangered • habitat • herbivore • vanish • irreplaceable •

1. The birthday gift Bertha's grandmother gave her is _____ .

2. Humans are bipeds while dogs and cats are _____ .

3. The bald eagle is no longer on the _____ species list.

4. The dodo, a species of flightless bird once native to New Zealand, has been _____ for over two hundred years.

5. Many think that the sasquatch, or "Big Foot," is an example of a yet undiscovered _____ living in the mountains of western North America.

6. The Amazon jungle, _____ for millions of animal species, is _____ at an alarming rate.

7. Scientists are learning that many types of cancer are caused by damaged _____ .

8. The chocolate cake Lisa made for the office party was so good it simply _____ .

9. An omnivore, such as the grizzly bear, is an animal that is both a carnivore and an _____ .

10. Domestic house cats are both diurnal and nocturnal; however, they are _____ nocturnal.

EXERCISE 15-C | Spelling Quiz – Track #15

Directions: √ Go to track #15 on CD #1.

√ For this quiz, you will hear a word, a phrase or an idiom. You will hear it twice. You will then have ten seconds to type it.

√ As you type the word(s), say each letter.

√ Check your answers in the word list on the previous page.

√ Record your score on page 201.

EXERCISE 15-D | 60-Word Typing Test

Directions: You have 60 seconds to type the following passage. When you are finished, calculate your wpm score. Record your score on page 201.

Mountain gorillas are endangered primates that inhabit the mountain forests of central Africa. They are primarily herbivores and are quadrupeds. They are very social with strong family bonds. Their DNA is 97.7 per cent the same as human DNA. Sadly, they are in danger of becoming extinct inasmuch as their habitat is vanishing. If they become extinct, they'll be irreplaceable.

WPM Score = _____ **/ 60**

Review #3

Directions: You have 60 seconds to complete this task. Do not use a dictionary. Check your answers on page 192. Record your score on page 201.

1. drought (n)

a. long period of no precipitation
b. long period of war
c. long period of peace
d. long period of creation

2. famine (n)

a. extreme lack of food
b. extreme lack of rain
c. extreme lack of land
d. extreme lack of work

3. reign (v)

a. to rule like a queen or king
b. to control for a time period
c. to exercise authority
d. all of the above

4. repeal (v)

a. to seek justice
b. to rescind officially
c. to make a deal
d. to repeat a deal

5. placid (adj)

a. mad and upset
b. calm and gentle
c. excited and restless
d. dangerous and evil

6. tsunami (n)

a. ocean waves caused by a ship
b. ocean wave caused by an earthquake
c. excellent surfing wave caused by a big storm
d. series of high ocean waves

7. go bankrupt (v)

a. to be able to pay one's bills
b. to be judged unable to pay one's bills
c. to forget a plethora of unpaid bills
d. free to pay no bills

8. aggregate (n)

a. big pieces broken into smaller pieces
b. many big and small pieces
c. too many broken pieces
d. small pieces joined to make a big piece

9. DNA (n)

a. deoxyribonucleic acid
b. the building blocks of life
c. genetic instructions
d. all of the above

10. extinct (adj)

a. species still living
b. species becoming fewer
c. species no longer living
d. species struggling to survive

EXERCISE 16-A Multiple-Choice Quiz

<u>Directions</u>: You have 2 minutes to complete this task. Do not use a dictionary. Check your answers on page 192. Record your score on page 201.

1. cosmos (n)

a. the planets
b. the oceans
c. the sky
d. the universe

2. galaxy (n)

a. massive group of stars
b. small group of moons
c. massive group of rivers
d. small group of planets

3. meteor (n)

a. small to large-sized rock
b. planet-sized object
c. flash of light
d. type of space ship

4. black hole (n)

a. massive invisible hole in space
b. massive visible hole in space
c. myriad holes on the moon
d. volcano

5. comet (n)

a. celestial body with a tail
b. celestial body with a moon
c. celestial body without a tail
d. celestial body with wings

6. asteroid (n)

a. small planet-sized rock
b. medium-sized meteor
c. large twin moons
d. small rock

7. wipe out (v)

a. to remove completely
b. to destroy completely
c. to eradicate
d. all of the above

8. orbit (v)

a. to travel through an object
b. to travel out of an object
c. to travel around an object
d. to travel inside an object

9. dinosaurs (n)

a. gigantic herbivore and carnivore reptiles of the Mesozoic Era
b. gigantic primates of the Jurassic Era
c. towering herbivore reptiles of the Triassic Period
d. extinct carnivores

10. cataclysmic (adj)

a. sudden and violent change
b. transformation
c. earth-changing event
d. all of the above

EXERCISE 16-B   Sentence-Completion Quiz

Directions: You have 5 minutes to complete this task. Check your answers on page 192. Record your score on page 201.

Word List   cosmos • galaxy • meteor • black hole • comet • asteroid • orbit • wipe out • dinosaurs • cataclysmic •

1. Earth is located in the _____ called the Milky Way.

2. _____ are one of the cosmos' greatest mysterious.

3. Since the dawn of time, man has looked up at the _____ and wondered what mysteries were out there.

4. The Indian Ocean Earthquake in December, 2004 was a _____ event.

5. Director Steven Spielberg popularized _____ in the movie *Jurassic Park*.

6. If you look up into the night sky, you can see satellites _____ the earth.

7. Overfishing is _____ fish stocks around the world.

8. Scientists are tracking _____ to make sure they do not hit the Earth.

9. A _____ shower is a group of meteors entering, and burning up, in the Earth's atmosphere.

10. In the Middle Ages, a _____ was seen as a bad omen.

EXERCISE 16-C Spelling Quiz – Track #16

Directions: √ Go to track #16 on CD #1.

√ For this quiz, you will hear a word, a phrase or an idiom. You will hear it twice. You will then have ten seconds to type it.

√ As you type the word(s), say each letter.

√ Check your answers in the word list on the previous page.

√ Record your score on page 201.

EXERCISE 16-D 60-Word Typing Test

Directions: You have 60 seconds to type the following passage. When you are finished, calculate your wpm score. Record your score on page 201.

Look up at the cosmos on a clear night. What do you see? You see the moon, stars and galaxies. You might even see a meteor or a comet. Far beyond human sight are black holes and asteroids. An asteroid is a big rock orbiting the sun. One hit Earth with such cataclysmic force that it wiped out the dinosaurs.

WPM Score =   **/ 60**

EXERCISE 17-A   Multiple-Choice Quiz

Directions: You have 2 minutes to complete this task. Do not use a dictionary.
Check your answers on page 192. Record your score on page 201.

1. ous (suffix)

a. meaning full of
b. meaning possessing
c. meaning having
d. all of the above

2. copious (adj)

a. a lot of
b. large number
c. abundant
d. all of the above

3. superfluous (adj)

a. unnecessary
b. excessive
c. useless
d. all of the above

4. ludicrous (adj)

a. stupid
b. ridiculous
c. not worth consideration
d. all of the above

5. comestible (n)

a. something edible
b. food
c. something to eat
d. all of the above

6. ravenous (adj)

a. really hungry
b. starving
c. famished
d. all of the above

7. miraculous (adj)

a. incredible
b. like a miracle
c. unbelievable
d. all of the above

8. punctilious (adj)

a. eye for detail
b. strict
c. formal
d. all of the above

9. diligent (adj)

a. hard-working
b. energetic
c. industrious
d. all of the above

10. on top of that (phr)

a. moreover
b. in addition
c. plus
d. all of the above

EXERCISE 17-B Sentence-Completion Quiz

<u>Directions</u>: You have 5 minutes to complete this task. Check your answers on page 192. Record your score on page 201.

<u>Words</u> <u>List</u>	ous • copious • superfluous • ludicrous • comestible • ravenous • miraculous • punctilious • diligent • on top of that •

1. After hibernating all winter, the mother grizzly bear was _____ .

2. The most _____ students will succeed.

3. Finding life on Mars would be _____ .

4. During the annual meeting, Surendra took _____ notes.

5. _____ is a common suffix in English.

6. Whenever Stephanie travels abroad, she likes to visit grocery stores to see what kind of _____ people are eating.

7. Amara scored a perfect 120 on the TOEFL test. _____ , she got a scholarship at Yale.

8. Have you ever noticed that Professor Morrison is very _____ ?

9. Miranda already has a great laptop, and she just bought another one. Talk about _____ .

10. My boss wants me to work Saturday and Sunday for no pay. That's _____ .

EXERCISE 17-C   Spelling Quiz – Track #17

Directions: √ Go to track #17 on CD #1.

√ For this quiz, you will hear a word, a phrase or an idiom. You will hear it twice. You will then have ten seconds to type it.

√ As you type the word(s), say each letter.

√ Check your answers in the word list on the previous page.

√ Record your score on page 201.

EXERCISE 17-D   60-Word Typing Test

Directions: You have 60 seconds to type the following passage. When you are finished, calculate your wpm score. Record your score on page 201.

Many English words end in the suffix ous. For example, if you're a diligent student, you undoubtedly take copious notes. On top of that, you're quite punctilious. Since you work hard, you're often ravenous and love delicious comestibles. You think buying expensive contrivances is superfluous and ludicrous, and a perfect TOEFL score would be wonderful, marvelous, not to mention miraculous.

WPM Score =   / 60

EXERCISE 18-A   Multiple-Choice Quiz

<u>**Directions**</u>: You have 2 minutes to complete this task. Do not use a dictionary. Check your answers on page 192. Record your score on page 201.

1. photosynthesis (n)

a. chemical energy into light energy
b. energy used for photography
c. plant energy into light energy
d. light energy into chemical energy

2. atmosphere (n)

a. gas surrounding a celestial body
b. gas in a galaxy
c. gas from comets and meteors
d. gas transformed into air

3. capture (v)

a. to catch and hold
b. to grab hold of
c. to take and hold
d. all of the above

4. chloroplast (n)

a. site of photosynthesis in a plant
b. a plethora of plant energy
c. recycled plant energy
d. light produced by a plant

5. convert (v)

a. to transform
b. to change
c. to alter
d. all of the above

6. whereby (conj)

a. on which
b. of which
c. in which
d. which is

7. absorb (v)

a. to take in
b. to receive
c. to consume
d. all of the above

8. molecule (n)

a. smallest part of something that still has the same properties
b. extremely small particle
c. particle containing two or more atoms
d. all of the above

9. organism (n)

a. unique life form
b. a group of life forms
c. individual life form
d. transforming life form

10. unique (adj)

a. special
b. original
c. one of a kind
d. all of the above

EXERCISE 18-B   Sentence-Completion Quiz

Directions: You have 5 minutes to complete this task. Check your answers on page 192. Record your score on page 201.

Word List	photosynthesis • atmosphere • capture • chloroplast • unique • whereby • absorb • molecule • organism • convert •

1. _____ is an integral part of photosynthesis.

2. Have you seen Justine's paintings? Her style is so _____ .

3. The _____ surrounding the Earth is approximately seventy-five miles thick.

4. Bruno likes _____ sunsets shimmering on the lake with his camera.

5. Mohamed wants _____ his house into apartments.

6. If there were no _____ , there would be no agrarian cultures.

7. In some cultures, marriage is an official process _____ a man and a woman agree to spend the rest of their lives together.

8. Finding living _____ on Mars would be miraculous.

9. Olga is an assiduous student; however, she will not be in TOEFL class tomorrow inasmuch as she needs more time _____ the writing strategies she learned in yesterday's class.

10. Alphonse has quite a fertile imagination. He says he can see a _____ with his own two eyes. Sorry, but I think that is ludicrous.

EXERCISE 18-C | Spelling Quiz – Track #18

Directions: √ Go to track #18 on CD #1.

√ For this quiz, you will hear a word, a phrase or an idiom. You will hear it twice. You will then have ten seconds to type it.

√ As you type the word(s), say each letter.

√ Check your answers in the word list on the previous page.

√ Record your score on page 201.

EXERCISE 18-D | 60-Word Typing Test

Directions: You have 60 seconds to type the following passage. When you are finished, calculate your wpm score. Record your score on page 201.

In plants, photosynthesis is the process whereby carbon dioxide is converted into sugar. First, chloroplast in the leaves absorbs sunlight to make ATP, a molecule which stores light energy. Next, ATP captures carbon dioxide from the atmosphere and converts it into carbohydrates, such as sugar. Plants are unique inasmuch as they're the only organisms that can make their own food.

WPM Score =   / 60

EXERCISE 19-A   Multiple-Choice Quiz

Directions: You have 2 minutes to complete this task. Do not use a dictionary.
Check your answers on page 192. Record your score on page 201.

1. precipitate (v)

a. to cause to happen
b. to bring about
c. to change from one state to another
d. all of the above

2. abolitionist (n)

a. one who wants abalone
b. one who wants to end something
c. one who wants to see something
d. one who wants nothing

3. cease (v)

a. to seize
b. to follow
c. to stop
d. to continue

4. label (v)

a. to put a name on
b. to insult someone
c. to cause injury to someone
d. to fight for justice

5. immoral (adj)

a. that which the group finds unreasonable
b. that which the group finds overwhelming
c. that which the group considers the wrong behavior
d. not which the group considers unintelligent

6. anathema (n)

a. idea or object of respect
b. idea or object of great joy
c. idea or object of fear
d. idea or object of great loathing

7. proposition (n)

a. idea to be debated
b. proposed plan
c. focus of an argument
d. all of the above

8. enflame (v)

a. to make happy
b. to make said
c. to make angry
d. to make excited

9. antipathy (n)

a. dislike for
b. agreement with
c. capable of
d. reason against

10. secession (n)

a. the act of joining
b. the process of acting
c. the process of leaving
d. the act of staying

EXERCISE 19-B   Sentence-Completion Quiz

Directions: You have 5 minutes to complete this task. Check your answers on page 192. Record your score on page 201.

Word List	precipitate • abolitionist • cease • label • immoral • enflame • anathema • proposition • antipathy • secession •

1. Farouk's idea of dropping out of university before graduating is _____ to his parents.

2. When it comes to soccer, there has always been great _____ between Brazil and Argentina.

3. In many ways, Martin Luther King was an _____ trying to emancipate blacks from white discrimination.

4. Sorry, but I think that Fernando's latest _____ for reducing the number of working hours per week is not feasible.

5. The idea that the government does not provide free public health insurance for everyone is _____ to many Americans.

6. When she was in high school, Elizabeth's friends _____ her a genius because she had such an astounding mind for numbers.

7. What _____ the fight between Al and Krissy? They seemed so happy.

8. In the 1970s, many French-speaking inhabitants of the province of Quebec shared the same dream: _____ from Canada.

9. The loud music in the apartment next door has finally _____ .

10. In 1765, the introduction of the Stamp Act, a direct tax on printed material and imposed on the American colonies by the British parliament, only _____ American _____ for the British.

EXERCISE 19-C   Spelling Quiz – Track #19

Directions: √ Go to track #19 on CD #1.

√ For this quiz, you will hear a word, a phrase or an idiom. You will hear it twice. You will then have ten seconds to type it.

√ As you type the word(s), say each letter.

√ Check your answers in the word list on the previous page.

√ Record your score on page 201.

EXERCISE 19-D   60-Word Typing Test

Directions: You have 60 seconds to type the following passage. When you are finished, calculate your wpm score. Record your score on page 201.

In 1860, the northern abolitionist proposition that owning slaves was immoral, and that it should cease, was anathema to southern slave-owning states who viewed slavery as a legal right based on state, not federal, law. The election of Abraham Lincoln, whom the south labeled an abolitionist, only enflamed southern antipathy to the north and precipitated the secession of southern states.

WPM Score =   / 60

EXERCISE 20-A Multiple-Choice Quiz

Directions: You have 2 minutes to complete this task. Do not use a dictionary. Check your answers on page 192. Record your score on page 201.

1. indigenous (adj)

a. native
b. foreign
c. related
d. enslaved

2. immunity (n)

a. rejection
b. protection
c. inspection
d. immigration

3. flourish (v)

a. to do nothing
b. to do adequately
c. to do poorly
d. to do very well

4. heretofore (adv)

a. previously
b. eventually
c. sequentially
d. here and there

5. exchange (v)

a. to regulate
b. to trade
c. to negotiate
d. to precipitate

6. monumental (adj)

a. astounding
b. large and impressive
c. extremely significant
d. all of the above

7. hence (adv)

a. therefore
b. believe or not
c. in contrast
d. indeed

8. devastating (adj)

a. to destroy
b. to shock and stun
c. to ruin completely
d. all of the above

9. launch (v)

a. to begin
b. to start
c. to commence
d. all of the above

10. era (n)

a. ancient time period
b. famous time period
c. specific time period
d. one hundred years

EXERCISE 20-B   Sentence-Completion Quiz

Directions: You have 5 minutes to complete this task. Check your answers on page 192. Record your score on page 201.

Word List	indigenous • immunity • flourish • heretofore • exchange • era • monumental • hence • devastating • launch •

1. Suffice it to say, the internet is a fast way to _____ information.

2. Meteorologists are predicting that three _____ hurricanes will hit Florida this year.

3. Eskimos are _____ to northern Canada and Alaska.

4. The destruction of the Berlin Wall was a _____ moment in world history.

5. That company always saturates the market with advertising whenever it _____ a new product.

6. The deer that inhabit the park are _____ because they have no natural predators.

7. The president keeps alluding to a problem _____ unknown to everyone in the company.

8. Lincoln emancipated the slaves _____ he is considered a _____ figure in American history.

9. The judge granted the witness _____ from prosecution.

10. Robert, Sally and Joe were all born in the _____ known as the Baby Boom.

EXERCISE 20-C | Spelling Quiz – Track #20

Directions: √ Go to track #20 on CD #1.

√ For this quiz, you will hear a word, a phrase or an idiom. You will hear it twice. You will then have ten seconds to type it.

√ As you type the word(s), say each letter.

√ Check your answers in the word list on the previous page.

√ Record your score on page 201.

EXERCISE 20-D | 60-Word Typing Test

Directions: You have 60 seconds to type the following passage. When you are finished, calculate your wpm score. Record your score on page 201.

> The Columbian Exchange was a monumental event in world history. It launched the east-west exchange of cultures and goods. The era commenced with Columbus' arrival in the New World, hence "Columbian Exchange." New diseases introduced to the old world flourished, devastating millions of indigenous people who had no immunity, while the tomato, a heretofore unknown fruit, was introduced to Europe.

WPM Score = / 60

Review #4

Directions: You have 60 seconds to complete this task. Do not use a dictionary. Check your answers on page 192. Record your score on page 201.

1. cataclysmic (adj)

a. sudden and violent change
b. transformation
c. earth-changing event
d. all of the above

2. copious (adj)

a. a lot of
b. large number
c. abundant
d. all of the above

3. heretofore (adv)

a. previously
b. eventually
c. sequentially
d. here and there

4. on top of that (phr)

a. moreover
b. in addition
c. plus
d. all of the above

5. whereby (conj)

a. on which
b. of which
c. in which
d. which is

6. orbit (v)

a. to travel through an object
b. to travel out of an object
c. to travel around an object
d. to travel inside an object

7. proposition (n)

a. idea to be debated
b. proposed plan
c. focus of an argument
d. all of the above

8. organism (n)

a. unique life form
b. a group of life forms
c. individual life form
d. transforming life form

9. precipitate (v)

a. to cause to happen
b. to bring about
c. to change from one state to another
d. all of the above

10. indigenous (adj)

a. native
b. foreign
c. related
d. enslaved

EXERCISE 21-A   Multiple-Choice Quiz

Directions: You have 2 minutes to complete this task. Do not use a dictionary. Check your answers on page 192. Record your score on page 201.

1. Catch-22 (id, n)

a. trapped by opposing conditions
b. situation preventing a solution to a problem
c. a no-win situation
d. all of the above

2. drop out of (v)

a. to quit
b. to leave
c. to end
d. all of the above

3. benefits (n)

a. conditions
b. guarantees
c. membership
d. advantages

4. perplexed (adj)

a. nonplused
b. confused
c. discombobulated
d. all of the above

5. it goes without saying (phr)

a. it is obvious
b. the facts are clear
c. as you can see
d. all of the above

6. persist with (v)

a. to stop
b. to remember
c. to avoid
d. to continue

7. counter (v)

a. to argue the opposite
b. to agree completely
c. to suggest often
d. to respond slowly

8. enumerate (v)

a. to enjoy a number of
b. to sell a number of
c. to buy a number of
d. to list the number of

9. pull the plug (id, v)

a. to end something
b. to empty a sink or bath by pulling the drain plug
c. to cut off
d. all of the above

10. quandary (n)

a. feeling of confidence
b. full of energy
c. feeling rested
d. unable to decide

EXERCISE 21-B   Sentence-Completion Quiz

Directions: You have 5 minutes to complete this task. Check your answers on page 192. Record your score on page 201.

Word List	Catch-22 • drop out of • benefits • perplexed • counter • it goes without saying • persist with • enumerate • quandary • pull the plug •

1. There are many _____ to speaking a foreign language.

2. The idiom _____ comes from the novel of the same name.

3. _____ that you should study for the TOEFL test.

4. Sylvia's boss _____ on her latest project inasmuch as it contained a plethora of problems.

5. When TOEFL test-takers choose a distractor, then realize they made a mistake, they are _____ because the distractor seemed correct.

6. Farouk abandoned his plans of becoming a doctor when he _____ med school.

7. Despite the poor economy, the company is _____ its plan to build ten new resorts.

8. Lily said that eating meat renders people fat and unhealthy. Edmund _____ by saying that man had to eat more than just vegetables to acquire enough daily protein.

9. Toni really wants to go back to Brazil, but he just got promoted to vice president of North American marketing. He is definitely in a _____ .

10. Last class, the professor _____ the ways you can get a high independent essay score.

EXERCISE 21-C | Spelling Quiz – Track #21

<u>Directions</u>: √ Go to track #21 on CD #1.

√ For this quiz, you will hear a word, a phrase or an idiom. You will hear it twice. You will then have ten seconds to type it.

√ As you type the word(s), say each letter.

√ Check your answers in the word list on the previous page.

√ Record your score on page 201.

EXERCISE 21-D | 60-Word Typing Test

<u>Directions</u>: You have 60 seconds to type the following passage. When you are finished, calculate your wpm score. Record your score on page 201.

Mary's in a Catch-22. She needs to drop out of school and get a job.

Yet if she doesn't get her degree, she won't get a job. Brian said Mary

should persist whereas Michelle countered by enumerating the

benefits of pulling the plug on school. It goes without saying that

Mary's in a quandary. She has never felt so perplexed.

WPM Score =   / 60

EXERCISE 22-A   Multiple-Choice Quiz

Directions: You have 2 minutes to complete this task. Do not use a dictionary. Check your answers on page 192. Record your score on page 201.

1. kill two birds with one stone (id, v)

a. to take control of one's future
b. to accomplish a myriad of things
c. to do two things at the same time
d. to solve difficult answers

2. the icing on the cake (id, n)

a. the best part
b. the amazing part
c. the good part
d. all of above

3. pull through with flying colors (id, v)

a. to fail beyond expectation
b. to succeed beyond expectation
c. to try one's best all the time
d. to succeed without trying

4. overwhelmed (adj)

a. feeling buried
b. feeling too much pressure
c. feeling out of control
d. all of the above

5. significant other (id)

a. friend
b. spouse
c. lover
d. superior

6. walk on air (id, v)

a. to be extremely light
b. to feel extremely airy
c. to be extremely happy
d. to feel extremely perplexed

7. blow away (id, v)

a. to be amazed
b. to be astounded
c. to feel shocked
d. all of the above

8. gratis (adj)

a. not free
b. free
c. with a tip
d. expensive

9. painstaking (adj)

a. difficult process
b. effortless process
c. discombobulating idea
d. copious process

10. loaded (id)

a. rich
b. poor
c. impecunious
d. overwhelmed

EXERCISE 22-B   Sentence-Completion Quiz

<u>Directions:</u> You have 5 minutes to complete this task. Check your answers on page 192. Record your score on page 201.

<u>Word</u> <u>List</u>	kill two birds with one stone • the icing on the cake • pull through with flying colors • overwhelmed • significant other • walk on air • blow away • gratis • painstaking • loaded •

1. Andrea was _____ when she learned that she was accepted into New York University.

2. Nicholas _____ when he went to the BMW dealer and bought two new BMWs: one for himself and one for his wife.

3. Peter always feels _____ at work inasmuch as he always has a plethora of things to do.

4. Climbing Mount Everest is not only extremely perilous but also a _____ process that can take years to complete.

5. It goes without saying that Bill Gates is _____ .

6. Raquel's _____ was looking quite perplexed when she said that she loved him but didn't want to marry him.

7. When the United States beats Brazil for the World Cup, I will be _____ .

8. Edgar was faced with a Catch-22. He wanted to accept the scholarship. It was _____ yet the low-ranked college was in the middle of nowhere.

9. Ken's surgery went just fine. He _____ .

10. I just won the lottery! _____ is it's tax free!

EXERCISE 22-C　　Spelling Quiz – Track #22

Directions: √ Go to track #22 on CD #1.

√ For this quiz, you will hear a word, a phrase or an idiom. You will hear it twice. You will then have ten seconds to type it.

√ As you type the word(s), say each letter.

√ Check your answers in the word list on the previous page.

√ Record your score on page 201.

EXERCISE 22-D　　60-Word Typing Test

Directions: You have 60 seconds to type the following passage. When you are finished, calculate your wpm score. Record your score on page 201.

Carmen killed two birds with one stone: she graduated with a medical and a law degree. It was painstaking, and she often felt overwhelmed, yet she pulled through with flying colors. Her friends were blown away, indeed, while Carmen was walking on air. The icing on the cake is her education was gratis inasmuch as her significant other is loaded.

WPM Score =　　　　/ 60

EXERCISE 23-A — Multiple-Choice Quiz

Directions: You have 2 minutes to complete this task. Do not use a dictionary. Check your answers on page 192. Record your score on page 201.

1. feel like a fish out of water
(id, v)

a. to be in the wrong place
b. to feel out of context
c. to know you do not fit in
d. all of the above

2. overcome (v)

a. to come together
b. to get better
c. to defeat
d. to go over

3. take the bull by the horns
(id, v)

a. to take control
b. to take responsibility
c. to face a challenge directly
d. all of the above

4. misgivings (n)

a. feelings of giving
b. feelings of doubt
c. feelings of fear
d. feelings of pride

5. pack it in (id)

a. to surrender
b. to quit
c. to pack one's bags and leave
d. all of the above

6. truly (adv)

a. really
b. indeed
c. yes
d. all of the above

7. cherish (v)

a. to share occasionally
b. to infer clearly
c. to value always
d. to avoid rarely

8. there and then (adv)

a. all in all
b. at that moment
c. in conclusion
d. at last

9. esteemed (adj)

a. loathed
b. respected
c. worshipped
d. fun

10. regard (n)

a. consideration for
b. respect for
c. attention to
d. all of the above

EXERCISE 23-B   Sentence-Completion Quiz

Directions: You have 5 minutes to complete this task. Check your answers on page 192. Record your score on page 201.

> Word List
>
> feel like a fish out of water • overcome • misgivings • truly •
> take the bull by the horns • pack it in • cherish • regard •
> esteemed • there and then •

1. Misako had _____ about getting married, so she decided to follow her best friend's advice and stay single.

2. That was the most amazing World Series I have ever seen, _____ .

3. Drunk drivers have no _____ for the safety of others.

4. Many peoples throughout history have had _____ the proposition that they were somehow inferior simply because they were indigenous.

5. The _____ doctor launched a devastating criticism of the current health care system.

6. If Sally _____ , she will finally get out of her quandary.

7. After a hard day at the office, Mary-Ann decided _____ .

8. Ricardo has always _____ his independence.

9. Miguel decided to go on a diet, _____ .

10. Aaliyah will always _____ in Manhattan.

EXERCISE 23-C	Spelling Quiz – Track #23

Directions: √ Go to track #23 on CD #1.

√ For this quiz, you will hear a word, a phrase or an idiom. You will hear it twice. You will then have ten seconds to type it.

√ As you type the word(s), say each letter.

√ Check your answers in the word list on the previous page.

√ Record your score on page 201.

EXERCISE 23-D	60-Word Typing Test

Directions: You have 60 seconds to type the following passage. When you are finished, calculate your wpm score. Record your score on page 201.

Truly, Bridget felt like a fish out of water the first day of class. She was so overwhelmed she wanted to pack it in, there and then. Yet she persisted and overcame her misgivings by taking the bull by the horns. In time, she came to cherish the immeasurable regard she had for her friends and for her esteemed professors.

WPM Score =   / 60

EXERCISE 24-A   Multiple-Choice Quiz

Directions: You have 2 minutes to complete this task. Do not use a dictionary. Check your answers on page 192. Record your score on page 201.

1. tion (suffix)

a. meaning action or reaction
b. meaning action or process
c. meaning action or contraction
d. meaning action or explanation

2. disintegration (n)

a. to disintegrate
b. to fall apart totally
c. to dissolve completely
d. all of the above

3. the $64,000.00 question (id, n)

a. the big question
b. the only question
c. the obvious question
d. all of the above

4. reincarnation (n)

a. end of light and time
b. rebirth after death
c. entering another world
d. process of awakening

5. figment (n)

a. statement of truth
b. piece of something broken
c. something imagined
d. delicious fruit

6. expiration (n)

a. end
b. death
c. termination
d. all of the above

7. contemplation (n)

a. act of thinking
b. act of baiting
c. act of tempting
d. act of conning

8. transfiguration (n)

a. change in shape or figure
b. change in appearance or look
c. process of transfiguring
d. all of the above

9. manifestation (n)

a. act of revealing
b. act of leaving
c. act of buying
d. act of knowing

10. address (v)

a.   to deal with
b.   to answer an issue
c.   to speak directly to
d.   all of the above

EXERCISE 24-B   Sentence-Completion Quiz

Directions: You have 5 minutes to complete this task. Check your answers on page 192. Record your score on page 201.

<u>Word</u>
<u>List</u>
tion • disintegration • the $64,000.00 question • reincarnation •
figment • expiration • contemplation • transfiguration •
manifestation • address •

1. In English, the suffix _____ added to a verb describes the action of that verb. For example, demonstration describes the act of demonstrating.

2. Do you know which issues the president will _____ in his speech tonight?

3. What will my TOEFL score be? That is _____ .

4. If _____ is indeed a miraculous event, what happens to our DNA? DNA, it would seem, is irreplaceable. Wouldn't you agree?

5. Catherine loves examining organisms under a microscope. Whenever she does, she is always deep in _____ .

6. Whistling while one works is often a _____ of contentment.

7. When a meteor enters Earth orbit, its _____ is guaranteed inasmuch as the Earth's atmosphere is like a wall of heat the meteor cannot penetrate.

8. How old is that milk? Check the _____ date, will you?

9. The story of J. K. Rowling is about the _____ of an impecunious writer into arguably the richest woman the world.

10. Look, I got 120 on the TOEFL test. It's not a _____ of my imagination. Look, I have the official score report to prove it.

EXERCISE 24-C   Spelling Quiz – Track #24

Directions: √ Go to track #24 on CD #1.

√ For this quiz, you will hear a word, a phrase or an idiom. You will hear it twice. You will then have ten seconds to type it.

√ As you type the word(s), say each letter.

√ Check your answers in the word list on the previous page.

√ Record your score on page 201.

EXERCISE 24-D   60-Word Typing Test

Directions: You have 60 seconds to type the following passage. When you are finished, calculate your wpm score. Record your score on page 201.

What happens upon our expiration? For many, that's the $64,000.00 question. Do we experience reincarnation or rapid disintegration into dust? Are angels manifestations of our heavenly transfiguration or merely figments of our imaginations? Many investigators have tried to resolve this issue only to end up empty handed. Suffice it to say, more contemplation is needed when addressing this fascinating topic.

WPM Score =   / 60

EXERCISE 25-A   Multiple-Choice Quiz

<u>Directions:</u> You have 2 minutes to complete this task. Do not use a dictionary. Check your answers on page 192. Record your score on page 201.

1. have one's ducks in a row
(id, v)

a. to manifest organization
b. to manifest chaos
c. to manifest determination
d. to manifest one's love of ducks

2. black and white (id, adj)

a. clear
b. no confusion
c. obvious choices
d. all of the above

3. resilient (adj)

a. weak
b. fun
c. tough
d. lazy

4. climb the corporate ladder
(id, v)

a. to advance quickly in a company
b. to sell ladders for a company
c. to enter a company finally
d. to work for a corporation

5. adage (n)

a. wise saying considered true
b. educational experience for all
c. quest for religious knowledge
d. personal code of behavior

6. the early bird gets the worm
(id, n)

a. hard work leads to success
b. birds are hard workers
c. one should get up early
d. practice makes one perfect

7. espouse (v)

a. to deny
b. to reject
c. to support
d. to blow away

8. the captain of one's own ship
(id, n)

a. one's own boss
b. one's own captain
c. one's own leader
d. all of the above

9. without a doubt (phr)

a. certainly
b. no question
c. clearly
d. all of the above

10. indefatigable (adj)

a. never excited
b. never bored
c. never tired
d. never knowing

EXERCISE 25-B   Sentence-Completion Quiz

Directions: You have 5 minutes to complete this task. Check your answers on page 192. Record your score on page 201.

> **Word List**   have one's ducks in a row • black and white • indefatigable •
> climb the corporate ladder • espouse • adage • resilient •
> the captain of one's own ship • without a doubt •
> the early bird gets the worm •

1. Perpetua believes in the adage " _____ ."

2. Virginia _____ the idea that the university book store should sell e-book text books in order help students save money.

3. The new influenza virus is _____ to the new vaccines.

4. The sun will rise tomorrow morning _____ .

5. Caroline is determined to be _____ .

6. Why is Gretchen so punctilious? Because she always _____ .

7. It goes without saying that if Tomoko keeps _____ , she will be president before she is thirty unless, of course, someone pulls the plug on her.

8. The situation couldn't be more _____ . It's definitely a Catch-22.

9. When Hernan wants to drop out of school, he always remembers Thomas Edison's _____ : "Genius is ninety-nine per cent perspiration and one per cent inspiration."

10. Joan flies all over the world doing business. She's really _____ .

EXERCISE 25-C   Spelling Quiz – Track #25

Directions: √   Go to track #25 on CD #1.

√   For this quiz, you will hear a word, a phrase or an idiom. You will hear it twice. You will then have ten seconds to type it.

√   As you type the word(s), say each letter.

√   Check your answers in the word list on the previous page.

√   Record your score on page 201.

EXERCISE 25-D   60-Word Typing Test

Directions: You have 60 seconds to type the following passage. When you are finished, calculate your wpm score. Record your score on page 201.

Wally always has his ducks in a row. Plus, he is so resilient and indefatigable. Without a doubt, he will quickly climb the corporate ladder until he is the captain of his own ship. What's the secret of his success? Simple. He sees the world in black and white. Moreover, he espouses the adage, "The early bird gets the worm."

WPM Score =   **/ 60**

Review #5

Directions: You have 60 seconds to complete this task. Do not use a dictionary. Check your answers on page 192. Record your score on page 201.

1. Catch-22 (id, n)

a. trapped by opposing conditions
b. situation preventing a solution to a problem
c. a no-win situation
d. all of the above

2. truly (adv)

a. really
b. indeed
c. yes
d. all of the above

3. kill two birds with one stone (id, v)

a. to take control of one's future
b. to accomplish a myriad of things
c. to do two things at the same time
d. to solve difficult answers

4. overwhelmed (adj)

a. feeling buried
b. feeling too much pressure
c. feeling out of control
d. all of the above

5. take the bull by the horns (id, v)

a. to take control
b. to take responsibility
c. to face a challenge directly
d. all of the above

6. regard (n)

a. consideration for
b. respect for
c. attention to
d. all of the above

7. manifestation (n)

a. the action of revealing
b. the action of leaving
c. the action of buying
d. the action of knowing

8. transfiguration (n)

a. change in shape or figure
b. change in appearance or look
c. process of transfiguring
d. all of the above

9. espouse (v)

a. to deny
b. to reject
c. to support
d. to blow away

10. resilient (adj)

a. weak
b. fun
c. tough
d. lazy

EXERCISE 26-A Multiple-Choice Quiz

Directions: You have 2 minutes to complete this task. Do not use a dictionary. Check your answers on page 192. Record your score on page 201.

1. contract (n)

a. agreement to perform
b. exchange of promises
c. legally binding agreement
d. all of the above

2. breach (v)

a. to form
b. to allow
c. to break
d. to borrow

3. remedy (n)

a. solution
b. resolution
c. substitution
d. institution

4. apoplectic (adj)

a. very sad
b. very happy
c. very angry
d. very widespread

5. get wind of the fact that (id, v)

a. to lose an argument
b. to receive information
c. to make a tough decision
d. to send news

6. jurisdiction (n)

a. territory where a law applies
b. place where lawyers meet
c. a court of law
d. room where a jury meets

7. negligent (adj)

a. careless
b. lacking attention to duty
c. failing to perform
d. all of the above

8. recourse (n)

a. choice
b. plan of action
c. direction to follow
d. all of the above

9. sue (v)

a. to seek money for damages
b. to repair with needle and thread
c. to review a contract
d. to ask a lawyer for advice

10. stipulated (adj)

a. item required by a contract
b. object in question
c. the agreed to point
d. all of the above

EXERCISE 26-B   Sentence-Completion Quiz

Directions: You have 5 minutes to complete this task. Check your answers on page 192. Record your score on page 201.

Word List	contract • breach • remedy • apoplectic • jurisdiction • sue • get wind of the fact that • negligent • recourse • stipulated •

1. Clara snubbed the latest _____ offer that gave her only a two per cent pay increase over five years.

2. Jurgen made a monumental mistake when he _____ the contract.

3. The _____ date of delivery was agreed to by both parties.

4. Jason has a unique _____ for the common cold.

5. When Mia _____ her assistant was gambling online with company money, Mia pulled the plug and fired him.

6. After the hurricane swept through town and devastated the Smith's house, their only _____ was to rebuild.

7. Hector was _____ when he _____ his bank had not been paying interest on his savings account for more than twenty years.

8. Just because we are in the wrong _____ doesn't mean that the company that breached the contract has legal immunity.

9. If you text message when you are driving, you're being criminally _____ .

10. _____ is only one of many recourses when seeking a legal remedy.

EXERCISE 26-C — Spelling Quiz – CD Disc #2

Directions: √ Go to track #1 on CD #2.

√ For this quiz, you will hear a word, a phrase or an idiom. You will hear it twice. You will then have ten seconds to type it.

√ As you type the word(s), say each letter.

√ Check your answers in the word list on the previous page.

√ Record your score on page 201.

EXERCISE 26-D — 60-Word Typing Test

Directions: You have 60 seconds to type the following passage. When you are finished, calculate your wpm score. Record your score on page 201.

Zoe was apoplectic when she got wind of the fact that her supplier had breached the contract by failing to deliver the stipulated parts. Zoe was resolved to sue and promptly called her lawyer who said that the negligent supplier was located in a different jurisdiction. The only recourse was to seek a remedy in California, the supplier's home base.

WPM Score =   / 60

EXERCISE 27-A   Multiple-Choice Quiz

Directions: You have 2 minutes to complete this task. Do not use a dictionary. Check your answers on page 192. Record your score on page 201.

1. mass production (phr)

a. made in small amounts
b. made in various amounts
c. made in great amounts
d. made when needed

2. seminal (adj)

a. the very last
b. the very first
c. a perfect copy
d. a masterpiece

3. mechanized (adj)

a. machine-based process
b. human-based process
c. animal-based process
d. learning-based process

4. genius (n)

a. extraordinary intelligence
b. one who lives in a bottle
c. building blocks of life
d. notorious

5. ism (suffix)

a. meaning the practice of
b. meaning the condition of
c. meaning the belief in
d. all of the above

6. affordable (adj)

a. attractive price
b. price one can pay
c. within one's price range
d. all of the above

7. assembly line (phr)

a. moving belt in a factory
b. conveyor belt in a factory
c. chain moving in a circle
d. all of the above

8. mass consumption (phr)

a. consumers buying a lot
b. consumers saving money
c. consumers accepting high prices
d. consumers working more hours

9. essentially (adv)

a. as a result
b. basically
c. in addition
d. as illustrated

10. substantially (adv)

a. greatly
b. not much
c. rarely
d. occasionally

EXERCISE 27-B   Sentence-Completion Quiz

Directions: You have 5 minutes to complete this task. Check your answers on page 192. Record your score on page 201.

Word List	ism • mass production • seminal • mechanized • genius • affordable • assembly line • mass consumption • essentially • substantially •

1. Words such as pragmatism, socialism and egalitarianism all end in the suffix _____ .

2. It's not unusual for a _____ to have a mercurial temper.

3. University text books would be more _____ if they were all ebooks.

4. _____ , a Catch-22 means that you are in a no-win situation.

5. The Apple iPod, a _____ portable music player, first hit the market in 2001.

6. Manufacturers worldwide can thank Henry Ford for creating and successfully applying the seminal manufacturing process known as _____ .

7. Expensive champagne is not made for _____ .

8. An _____ accelerates the manufacturing process.

9. Cho He Lee retook the TOEFL test and _____ increased her score.

10. We live in a highly _____ world.

EXERCISE 27-C   Spelling Quiz – Track #2

Directions: √ Go to track #2 on CD #2.

√ For this quiz, you will hear a word, a phrase or an idiom. You will hear it twice. You will then have ten seconds to type it.

√ As you type the word(s), say each letter.

√ Check your answers in the word list on the previous page.

√ Record your score on page 201.

EXERCISE 27-D   60-Word Typing Test

Directions: You have 60 seconds to type the following passage. When you are finished, calculate your wpm score. Record your score on page 201.

The genius Henry Ford gave the world Fordism. Fordism is essentially the mass production of cars in a factory. As the cars move along an assembly line, each worker puts on a part. This seminal, mechanized process decreased production time and lowered costs substantially. The car, the Model-T, was so affordable everybody wanted one. This, in turn, created mass consumption.

WPM Score =   / 60

EXERCISE 28-A Multiple-Choice Quiz

Directions: You have 2 minutes to complete this task. Do not use a dictionary. Check your answers on page 192. Record your score on page 201.

1. originate in (v)

a. to start in
b. to exit in
c. to come in
d. to end in

2. fatigue (n)

a. intelligence
b. exhaustion
c. exactitude
d. fatuous

3. transmit (v)

a. to pass on
b. to spread
c. to send
d. all of the above

4. epidemic (n)

a. disease widespread locally
b. disease transforming
c. disease getting worse
d. disease killing many

5. pandemic (n)

a. disease under control
b. disease from apes
c. disease known as "the flu"
d. disease widespread globally

6. strain (n)

a. none of
b. type of
c. friend of
d. some of

7. poultry (n)

a. pigs and sheep
b. cows and horses
c. chickens and turkeys
d. cars and trucks

8. infectious (adj)

a. easily bought
b. easily learned
c. easily spread
d. easily fixed

9. symptom (n)

a. sign
b. indication
c. evidence
d. all of the above

10. virulent (adj)

a. deadly
b. harmless
c. friendly
d. mercurial

EXERCISE 28-B Sentence-Completion Quiz

Directions: You have 5 minutes to complete this task. Check your answers on page 192. Record your score on page 201.

> **Word List** originate in • fatigue • transmit • epidemic • pandemic • strain • poultry • infectious • symptoms • virulent •

1. Joan is a vegan hence she eschews _____ .

2. _____ is analogous to epidemic but on a worldwide scale.

3. The Spanish influenza of 1919 was extremely _____ , killing over 50 million people worldwide.

4. A flu _____ can quickly turn into a _____ .

5. After a hard day of work, Ryan feels really _____ .

6. Every year doctors have to deal with new _____ of influenza.

7. Natia had _____ of the flu, so she decided to call in sick.

8. Rubens' salary is _____ electronically into his bank account once every two weeks.

9. Because the flu is so _____ , it is a good idea to wash your hands whenever you can.

10. The personal computer, the micro processor, and the internet all _____ the United States.

| EXERCISE 28-C | Spelling Quiz – Track #3 |

Directions: √ Go to track #3 on CD #2.

√ For this quiz, you will hear a word, a phrase or an idiom. You will hear it twice. You will then have ten seconds to type it.

√ As you type the word(s), say each letter.

√ Check your answers in the word list on the previous page.

√ Record your score on page 201.

| EXERCISE 28-D | 60-Word Typing Test |

Directions: You have 60 seconds to type the following passage. When you are finished, calculate your wpm score. Record your score on page 201.

Influenza or "flu" is a highly infectious disease that originates in pigs and poultry, and is then transmitted to humans. The symptoms are chills, severe headaches and fatigue. The flu is a seasonal epidemic that can quickly turn into a global pandemic. In 1918 the Spanish Flu, a strain of pig flu, was particularly virulent, killing over 50 million people.

WPM Score = / 60

EXERCISE 29-A   Multiple-Choice Quiz

Directions: You have 2 minutes to complete this task. Do not use a dictionary. Check your answers on page 192. Record your score on page 201.

1. behemoth (n/adj)

a. huge
b. massive
c. monstrous
d. all of the above

2. symbol (n)

a. sign with meaning
b. sign with no meaning
c. sign with symptoms
d. miraculous sign

3. indomitable (adj)

a. can be conquered
b. cannot be conquered
c. will be conquered
d. often conquered

4. doomed (adj)

a. destined to reappear
b. destined to disappear
c. eventual awakening
d. destined to work hard

5. susceptible (adj)

a. open to
b. vulnerable to
c. defenseless
d. all of the above

6. coalesce (v)

a. to break apart
b. to come together as one
c. to borrow from others
d. to separate and return

7. frigid (adj)

a. very wet
b. very mild
c. very cold
d. very hot

8. perish (v)

a. to die
b. to vanish
c. to disappear
d. all of the above

9. owing to the fact that (adv)

a. because
b. since
c. inasmuch as
d. all of the above

10. tragic (adj)

a. great misfortune
b. disaster
c. cataclysmic
d. all of above

EXERCISE 29-B   Sentence-Completion Quiz

<u>Directions</u>: You have 5 minutes to complete this task. Check your answers on page 192. Record your score on page 201.

<u>Word</u> <u>List</u>	behemoth • symbol • indomitable • doomed • susceptible • coalesce • frigid • perished • owing to the fact that • tragic •

1. _____ is not analogous to cymbal.

2. Sybil quickly climbed the corporate ladder _____ she worked assiduously.

3. The old and the weak are more _____ to infectious diseases.

4. At over 170 tons, the blue whale, the largest animal on Earth, is a _____ .

5. Vincent Van Gogh, a seminal nineteenth century Dutch painter, died a _____ death.

6. It goes without saying that the polar bear is _____ if global warming continues to melt the ice at the North Pole at the current rate.

7. Tom's _____ spirit is infectious.

8. It is simply astounding that some organisms can reproduce in profuse numbers while inhabiting _____ environs.

9. The music of The Beatles illustrates how four great minds can _____ to create music the world regards as genius.

10. Many explorers have _____ while seeking new lands.

| EXERCISE 29-C | Spelling Quiz – Track #4 |

Directions: √ Go to track #4 on CD #2.

    √ For this quiz, you will hear a word, a phrase or an idiom. You will hear it twice. You will then have ten seconds to type it.

    √ As you type the word(s), say each letter.

    √ Check your answers in the word list on the previous page.

    √ Record your score on page 201.

| EXERCISE 29-D | 60-Word Typing Test |

Directions: You have 60 seconds to type the following passage. When you are finished, calculate your wpm score. Record your score on page 201.

Titanic was a symbol of man's indomitable spirit. At 46,328 tons, she was a behemoth in which the most advanced technology of the day had coalesced. Yet she was doomed owing to the fact that her hull, made of inferior iron, was susceptible to cracking in cold weather. Tragically, 1,517 out of 2,223 passengers perished in the frigid North Atlantic.

WPM Score =   / 60

EXERCISE 30-A | Multiple-Choice Quiz

<u>Directions</u>: You have 2 minutes to complete this task. Do not use a dictionary. Check your answers on page 192. Record your score on page 201.

1. founder (n)

a. one who starts a venture
b. one who is lost and found
c. one who finds things
d. one who breeds dogs

2. iconic (adj)

a. symbol of
b. sign of
c. representation of
d. all of the above

3. garage (n)

a. enclosed space for food
b. open space for a horse
c. enclosed space for a car
d. enclosed space for studying

4. genesis (n)

a. the end of
b. the middle of
c. the climax of
d. the beginning of

5. arguably (adv)

a. that which can be argued
b. that which was argued
c. that which will be argued
d. that which will discombobulate

6. incorporate (v)

a. to go bankrupt
b. to become a public company
c. to become a private company
d. to target a specific market

7. take root (v)

a. to end
b. to begin to grow
c. to quest
d. to take the bull by the horns

8. crucible (n)

a. place where forces meet
b. place of great heat
c. bowl used for melting objects
d. all of the above

9. inventiveness (n)

a. good at creating
b. ability to invent
c. talent for making new things
d. all of the above

10. moreover (adv)

a. in addition
b. in contrast
c. however
d. it goes with saying

EXERCISE 30-B   Sentence-Completion Quiz

Directions: You have 5 minutes to complete this task. Check your answers on page 192. Record your score on page 201.

Word List	founder • iconic • garage • genesis • arguably • incorporate • take root • crucible • inventiveness • moreover •

1. The seeds that Birgit germinated and planted have _____ .

2. American universities, such as Cal Tech and M.I.T., are _____ of seminal thought.

3. Thomas Edison was the _____ of the present-day conglomerate, General Electric.

4. TOEFL is , _____ , the most challenging English-language proficiency test in the world.

5. Some opulent houses in California have ten _____ .

6. The _____ of that novel was the manifestation of a ghost the author saw while reading about the *Titanic*.

7. American corporations place a high value on employee _____ .

8. If the founders of a private company do not want to be personally sued for a breach of contract, they should _____ .

9. Nick was not at school today. _____ , he did not come home last night.

10. Pele is an _____ sports figure.

EXERCISE 30-C   Spelling Quiz – Track #5

Directions: √ Go to track #5 on CD #2.

> √ For this quiz, you will hear a word, a phrase or an idiom. You will hear it twice. You will then have ten seconds to type it.

> √ As you type the word(s), say each letter.

> √ Check your answers in the word list on the previous page.

> √ Record your score on page 201.

EXERCISE 30-D   60-Word Typing Test

Directions: You have 60 seconds to type the following passage. When you are finished, calculate your wpm score. Record your score on page 201.

Great things happen in American garages. Apple had its genesis in a garage in the late 1970s while Google co-founders Larry Page and Sergei Brin incorporated Google in a garage in 1998. Moreover, almost every iconic American rock band has taken root in a garage, a creative crucible in which, arguably, American inventiveness is born and flourishes to this day.

WPM Score =   / 60

Review #6

Directions: You have 60 seconds to complete this task. Do not use a dictionary. Check your answers on page 192. Record your score on page 201.

1. remedy (n)

a. solution
b. resolution
c. substitution
d. institution

2. essentially (adv)

a. as a result
b. basically
c. in addition
d. as illustrated

3. epidemic (n)

a. disease widespread locally
b. disease transforming
c. disease getting worse
d. disease killing many

4. behemoth (n/adj)

a. huge
b. massive
c. monstrous
d. all of the above

5. coalesce (v)

a. to break apart
b. to borrow from others
c. to separate and return
d. to come together as one

6. genesis (n)

a. the end of
b. the middle of
c. the climax of
d. the beginning of

7. moreover (adv)

a. in addition
b. in contrast
c. however
d. it goes with saying

8. symptom (n)

a. sign
b. indication
c. evidence
d. all of the above

9. mechanized (adj)

a. machine-based process
b. human-based process
c. animal-based process
d. learning-based process

10. contract (n)

a. agreement to perform
b. exchange of promises
c. legally binding agreement
d. all of the above

EXERCISE 31-A   Multiple-Choice Quiz

Directions: You have 2 minutes to complete this task. Do not use a dictionary. Check your answers on page 192. Record your score on page 201.

1. frontier (n)

a. where civilization ends
b. border
c. point of transition
d. all of the above

2. savage (adj)

a. friendly
b. widespread
c. destructive
d. mercurial

3. jack-of-all-trades (id, adj)

a. can do only one thing well
b. genius at many things
c. can do many things well
d. likes to help others

4. quintessential (adj)

a. the best example
b. the perfect example
c. the most illustrative example
d. all of the above

5. herd (v)

a. to tie together
b. to learn together
c. to group together
d. to build together

6. none more so than (phr)

a. there is no better example
b. there is no example
c. there is a greater preference for
d. there is a better example

7. rugged (adj)

a. tough
b. hard
c. resolute
d. all of the above

8. self-reliant (adj)

a. dependent
b. selfish
c. lonely
d. independent

9. archetype (n)

a. original model or type
b. typical example or type
c. oldest symbol or type
d. symbol with many meanings

10. sublime (adj)

a.   god-like beauty
b.   god-like teaching
c.   god-like warning
d.   god-like understanding

EXERCISE 31-B   Sentence-Completion Quiz

Directions: You have 5 minutes to complete this task. Check your answers on page 192. Record your score on page 201.

Word List	frontier • savage • jack-of-all-trades • quintessential • herd • none more so than • rugged • self-reliant • archetype • sublime •

1. America has many famous presidents, _____ Abraham Lincoln.

2. It goes without saying that space is the new _____ .

3. What is the _____ dish or food of your country?

4. If you want to climb the corporate ladder, you must be _____ and a team player at the same time.

5. Al Capone was not only notorious and nefarious, but also the _____ American gangster.

6. The Rocky Mountains manifest a _____ beauty.

7. _____ individuals are not afraid to take the bull by the horns.

8. The job of a sheep dog is to _____ sheep.

9. Mona can fix anything. She is a _____ .

10. The frost last night _____ this year's orange crop.

EXERCISE 31-C	Spelling Quiz – Track #6

Directions: √ Go to track #6 on CD #2.

√ For this quiz, you will hear a word, a phrase or an idiom. You will hear it twice. You will then have ten seconds to type it.

√ As you type the word(s), say each letter.

√ Check your answers in the word list on the previous page.

√ Record your score on page 201.

EXERCISE 31-D	60-Word Typing Test

Directions: You have 60 seconds to type the following passage. When you are finished, calculate your wpm score. Record your score on page 201.

The American west was fertile ground for rugged individuals, none more so than the American cowboy. Truly, the cowboy is the quintessential American archetype; a rugged, self-reliant jack-of-all-trades inhabiting a vast frontier that was both savage and sublime. His main job was to herd cattle destined for Chicago's meat packing industry serving the growing demand for meat in the east.

WPM Score = _____ / 60

EXERCISE 32-A   Multiple-Choice Quiz

Directions: You have 2 minutes to complete this task. Do not use a dictionary.
Check your answers on page 192. Record your score on page 201.

1. pod (n)

a. small group of whales
b. small group of seals
c. small group of dolphins
d. all of the above

2. orca (n)

a. shark
b. whale
c. killer whale
d. rock band

3. apex predator (phr)

a. endangered carnivore
b. top carnivore
c. typical carnivore
d. extinct carnivore

4. matrilineal (adj)

a. following the father
b. following the brother
c. following the sister
d. following the mother

5. resident (n)

a. living in one place
b. living in various places
c. living alone
d. living dangerously

6. transient (adj)

a. one who stays in one place
b. one who always moves about
c. one who eschews trains
d. one who enjoys traveling

7. contrary to popular belief
(phr)

a. against what is true
b. agree with what is true
c. what most think
d. all of the above

8. appellation (n)

a. vision
b. champagne
c. garden
d. name

9. stocky (adj)

a. long and thin
b. short and heavy
c. long and wide
d. short and thin

10. life span (phr)

a. the length of a year
b. the length of a lunar month
c. the length of a life
d. the length of a summer day

EXERCISE 32-B — Sentence-Completion Quiz

Directions: You have 5 minutes to complete this task. Check your answers on page 192. Record your score on page 201.

<u>Word List</u>   pod • orca • apex predator • matrilineal • resident • transient • contrary to popular belief • appellation • stocky • life span •

---

1. Indeed, an iPod and a killer whale _____ are, in many ways, analogous. Both are related groups, one of music, one of killer whales. Moreover, both are a form of communication and protection.

2. The _____ of a Galapagos tortoise is simply astounding. Some are as old as 150 years.

3. Vancouver Island, with its sublime and rugged beauty, is a good place to view _____ in the wild.

4. The Great White shark is not only an _____ , but is also what many believe to be the quintessential shark.

5. _____ , you cannot pass or fail the TOEFL test. You simply receive a score that measures your English-language proficiency.

6. Some ancient agrarian societies were indeed _____ ; however, most were patrilineal.

7. The penguin is a not a _____ of the Arctic but of Antarctica.

8. Every type of wine has its own unique _____ .

9. Many herbivores are _____ owing to the fact that they must migrate great distances to find new sources of food.

10. Michael Jackson was not _____ . On the contrary, he was tall and quite thin.

EXERCISE 32-C	Spelling Quiz – Track #7

Directions: √ Go to track #7 on CD #2.

√ For this quiz, you will hear a word, a phrase or an idiom. You will hear it twice. You will then have ten seconds to type it.

√ As you type the word(s), say each letter.

√ Check your answers in the word list on the previous page.

√ Record your score on page 201.

EXERCISE 32-D	60-Word Typing Test

Directions: You have 60 seconds to type the following passage. When you are finished, calculate your wpm score. Record your score on page 201.

Contrary to popular belief, killer whales, or orcas, are not whales but highly intelligent dolphins. They have stocky, black-and-white bodies and travel in pods which are matrilineal. Orcas are apex predators, eating everything from fish to whales. They have a 50-year life span and have three distinct social patterns: transient, resident and offshore. Orca, a Roman appellation, means sea monster.

WPM Score =   / 60

EXERCISE 33-A Multiple-Choice Quiz

Directions: You have 2 minutes to complete this task. Do not use a dictionary. Check your answers on page 192. Record your score on page 201.

1. martyr (n)

a. dying for one's religious beliefs
b. dying for friends and family
c. dying for love of country
d. dying in a war

2. assassinate (v)

a. to kill for family reasons
b. to kill for business reasons
c. to kill for educational reasons
d. to kill for political reasons

3. ratify (v)

a. to approve
b. to confirm
c. to put your stamp on
d. all of the above

4. absolute (adj)

a. pure
b. not limited
c. total control
d. all of the above

5. archbishop (n)

a. Christian leader
b. Christian martyr
c. Christian teachings
d. religious army

6. venerate (v)

a. to worship
b. to treat like a friend
c. to loathe
d. all of the above

7. tyrannical (adj)

a. like a benevolent leader
b. like a tyrant
c. like teacher
d. like a company founder

8. confound (v)

a. to frustrate
b. to organize
c. to conclude
d. to coalesce

9. apace (adv)

a. essentially lazy with no purpose
b. slowly with no purpose
c. rapidly with purpose
d. all of the above

10. saint (n)

a. holy person
b. symbol of light
c. sign of divine power on earth
d. all of the above

EXERCISE 33-B Sentence-Completion Quiz

Directions: You have 5 minutes to complete this task. Check your answers on page 192. Record your score on page 201.

Word List	martyr • assassinate • ratify • absolute • archbishop • saint • venerate • tyrannical • confound • apace •

1. Millions were devastated when President John F. Kennedy was _____ in November of 1963.

2. Andrea cherishes and _____ her parents.

3. The United States and many other nations have yet to _____ the Kyoto Protocol, an international treaty addressing the issue of global warming.

4. A famous political adage states that "_____ power corrupts absolutely."

5. The researchers were continually _____ in their search to develop a vaccine for the virulent new strain of influenza.

6. Even though Chiyoko felt like a fish out of water when she first arrived in the United States, she nonetheless proceeded _____ to Columbia University where she would study for the next four years.

7. Morgan was feeling overwhelmed by the math homework so she asked Bob for help. He showed her a fast and easy way to answer each question. Morgan was so impressed she called him a _____ .

8. An _____ has a myriad of religious responsibilities.

9. Back in high school, Sung Hyo had a _____ English teacher.

10. A _____ must be resolute in his or her beliefs because the choice is, without a doubt, black and white.

EXERCISE 33-C   Spelling Quiz – Track #8

Directions: √ Go to track #8 on CD #2.

√ For this quiz, you will hear a word, a phrase or an idiom. You will hear it twice. You will then have ten seconds to type it.

√ As you type the word(s), say each letter.

√ Check your answers in the word list on the previous page.

√ Record your score on page 201.

EXERCISE 33-D   60-Word Typing Test

Directions: You have 60 seconds to type the following passage. When you are finished, calculate your wpm score. Record your score on page 201.

In 1170, Thomas Becket, Archbishop of Canterbury, was assassinated by men loyal to King Henry II. Tyrannical Henry wanted absolute rule over state and church; however, Becket confounded Henry's plans by refusing to ratify them. Apoplectic, Henry wished Becket dead. Men loyal to the king proceeded apace. Since then, Beckett has been canonized and venerated as a martyr and saint.

WPM Score =   / 60

EXERCISE 34-A   Multiple-Choice Quiz

Directions: You have 2 minutes to complete this task. Do not use a dictionary. Check your answers on page 192. Record your score on page 201.

1. burn the candle at both ends (id, v)

a. to work late and long
b. to burn candles for an experiment
c. to keep two fires burning at night
d. to keep warm with two candles

2. come with the territory (id, v)

a. to be a piece of cake
b. to be a plethora of responsibility
c. to be part of the job
d. to make a new start

3. put one's nose to the grindstone (id, v)

a. to focus on what is important
b. to avoid responsibility
c. to work in a factory
d. to innovate

4. ace (v)

a. to lose by a lot
b. to do extremely well
c. to give up without a fight
d. to play tennis

5. keep one's eye on the prize (id, v)

a. to fail to win a prize
b. to remember those you prize
c. to have a talent for winning
d. to focus always on what you are working for

6. push the envelope (id, v)

a. to mail a letter
b. to go to the extreme
c. to buy and sell paper
d. to go slow and carefully

7. give it one's best shot (id, v)

a. to feel devastated
b. to feel overwhelmed
c. to try to hit someone
d. to try one's best

8. conviction (n)

a. strong conflict
b. strong contract
c. strong fear
d. strong belief

9. kick back (id, v)

a. to take it easy
b. to take a job
c. to get back
d. to get a test result back

10. R and R (n)

a.   railroad
b.   rich and richer
c.   rest and relaxation
d.   right and righter

EXERCISE 34-B   Sentence-Completion Quiz

<u>Directions</u>: You have 5 minutes to complete this task. Check your answers on page 192. Record your score on page 201.

<u>Word</u> <u>List</u>	burn the candle at both ends • come with the territory • put one's nose to the grindstone • ace • push the envelope • keep one's eye on the prize • give it one's best shot • conviction • kick back • R and R •

1. Living on the American frontier meant there was a good chance you'd see, maybe even come into conflict with, Native Americans. That possibility _____ .

2. Will is indefatigable. He exercises every day for four hours. This Saturday, he's really going to _____ and exercise for eight hours straight.

3. At the end of each semester most students, overwhelmed by exams, are ready for a little _____ .

4. Pamela is of the _____ that the disease originated in poultry.

5. Mary has two exams tomorrow. Tonight, she really has to _____ .

6. Zinedine quickly climbed the corporate ladder by _____ .

7. It goes without saying that Hristo _____ the physics exam.

8. When Faye _____ , she likes to travel to affordable places.

9. When Henry Ford was developing the idea of Fordism, he never failed _____ : an affordable car everyone could own.

10. This text book has been designed to help you _____ the TOEFL test _____ .

EXERCISE 34-C — Spelling Quiz – Track #9

Directions: √ Go to track #9 on CD #2.

√ For this quiz, you will hear a word, a phrase or an idiom. You will hear it twice. You will then have ten seconds to type it.

√ As you type the word(s), say each letter.

√ Check your answers in the word list on the previous page.

√ Record your score on page 201.

EXERCISE 34-D — 60-Word Typing Test

Directions: You have 60 seconds to type the following passage. When you are finished, calculate your wpm score. Record your score on page 201.

Dalia's burning the candle at both ends because she wants to ace the TOEFL test. With absolute conviction, she knows that putting her nose to the grindstone comes with the territory. Even though she's pushing the envelope, she's keeping her eye on the prize. Test day, she'll give it her best shot, then kick back with some R and R.

WPM Score =   / 60

EXERCISE 35-A Multiple-Choice Quiz

Directions: You have 2 minutes to complete this task. Do not use a dictionary. Check your answers on page 192. Record your score on page 201.

1. ic (suffix)

a. meaning the nature of
b. meaning the time of
c. meaning the place of
d. meaning the origin of

2. romantic (adj)

a. unrealistic
b. guided by emotions
c. passionate
d. all of the above

3. pragmatic (adj)

a. prefers logic to emotion
b. practical
c. black and white
d. all of the above

4. enigmatic (adj)

a. frigid
b. mysterious
c. basic
d. friendly

5. have both feet on the ground
(id, v)

a. to be pragmatic
b. to feel romantic
c. to be unrealistic
d. to be enigmatic

6. cynic (adj)

a. one who trusts selfless acts
b. one who believes in religion
c. one who does not trust selfless acts
d. one who enjoys family life

7. have one's head in the clouds
(id, v)

a. to be cynical
b. to be a realist
c. to feel romantic
d. to be pragmatic

8. very much the (adv)

a. definitely
b. totally
c. really
d. all of the above

9. what one would call (phr)

a. an example of
b. a definition of
c. an illustration of
d. all of the above

10. diehard (adj)

a. overwhelmed
b. discombobulated
c. resolute
d. savage

EXERCISE 35-B   Sentence-Completion Quiz

Directions: You have 5 minutes to complete this task. Check your answers on page 192. Record your score on page 201.

> Word
> List
>
> ic • romantic • pragmatic • enigmatic • cynic • very much the •
> have one's feet on the ground • what one would call • diehard •
> have one's head in the clouds •

1. The suffix _____ means "having the nature of." Hence, if you are phlegmatic, you are stolid which, in turn, means void of emotion.

2. Larissa is a _____ soccer fan.

3. Women generally eschew action movies for _____ ones.

4. Mila is very _____ . She would love an opulent house but prefers to live in one she can afford.

5. Jim is also very pragmatic. He too has _____ .

6. Cyrus is _____ assiduous student.

7. Is Bread really the best appellation for a child? If you ask me, it sounds like the parents _____ when they chose that name.

8. Don't bother giving Cal a birthday present. He's a diehard _____ .

9. Bill Gates is _____ loaded.

10. Shakespeare's Hamlet is an _____ and tragic character.

| EXERCISE 35-C | Spelling Quiz – Track #10 |

Directions: √ Go to track #10 on CD #2.

√ For this quiz, you will hear a word, a phrase or an idiom. You will hear it twice. You will then have ten seconds to type it.

√ As you type the word(s), say each letter.

√ Check your answers in the word list on the previous page.

√ Record your score on page 201.

| EXERCISE 35-D | 60-Word Typing Test |

Directions: You have 60 seconds to type the following passage. When you are finished, calculate your wpm score. Record your score on page 201.

Samantha is very much the cynic, always doubting every little act of kindness whereas Carrie's a diehard romantic. She always has her head in the clouds. Charlotte, on other the hand, is very pragmatic. She definitely has her feet on the ground. As for Miranda, she's what I would call enigmatic. You never know what's going on inside her head.

WPM Score =   **/ 60**

Review #7

Directions: You have 60 seconds to complete this task. Do not use a dictionary. Check your answers on page 192. Record your score on page 201.

1. very much the (adv)

a. definitely
b. totally
c. completely
d. all of the above

2. push the envelope (id, v)

a. to mail a letter
b. to go to the extreme
c. to buy and sell paper
d. to go slow and carefully

3. ratify (v)

a. to approve
b. to confirm
c. to put your stamp on
d. all of the above

4. contrary to popular belief (phr)

a. against what is true
b. agree with what is true
c. what most think
d. all of the above

5. frontier (n)

a. where civilization ends
b. border
c. point of transition
d. all of the above

6. archetype (adj)

a. original model or type
b. typical example or type
c. oldest symbol or type
d. symbol with many meanings

7. apex predator (phr)

a. endangered carnivore
b. top carnivore
c. typical carnivore
d. extinct carnivore

8. confound (v)

a. to frustrate
b. to organize
c. to conclude
d. to coalesce

9. conviction (n)

a. strong conflict
b. strong contract
c. strong fear
d. strong belief

10. cynic (adj)

a. one who trusts selfless acts
b. one who believes in religion
c. one who does not trust selfless acts
d. one who enjoys family life

EXERCISE 36-A | Multiple-Choice Quiz

Directions: You have 2 minutes to complete this task. Do not use a dictionary. Check your answers on page 192. Record your score on page 201.

1. advent of (phr)

a. introduction of
b. development of
c. invention of
d. all of the above

2. concurrent with (phr)

a. simultaneously
b. unfortunately
c. consequently
d. conditionally

3. wayward (adj)

a. lost
b. innocent
c. placid
d. unerring

4. boom (n)

a. explosion
b. rapid expansion
c. fast growth
d. all of the above

5. wholesale (adj)

a. complete
b. total
c. utter
d. all of the above

6. specious (adj)

a. sounds convincing but lacks logic
b. sounds convincing and logical
c. sounds logical and important
d. sounds logical and esteemed

7. emblematic (adj)

a. symbolic of
b. sign of
c. indication of
d. all of the above

8. malefaction (n)

a. crime
b. violation
c. lawlessness
d. all of the above

9. brazen (adj)

a. shameless
b. shameful
c. shamed
d. shy

10. parasitic (adj)

a. benefiting by working with another
b. benefiting from another's hard work
c. benefiting with no effort
d. all of the above

EXERCISE 36-B   Sentence-Completion Quiz

Directions: You have 5 minutes to complete this task. Check your answers on page 192. Record your score on page 201.

Word List	advent of • concurrent with • wayward • boom • wholesale • specious • emblematic • malefaction • brazen • parasitic •

1. Fleas are considered _____ because they live off the blood of cats and dogs, as well as a myriad of other mammals.

2. The _____ Fordism also brought about the _____ mass consumption.

3. Mass consumption is _____ of a consumer society that either has a lot of cash in the form of money or is subsisting primarily on credit, or both.

4. The opposite of _____ is bust.

5. The _____ son finally found his way home.

6. The tsunami's _____ destruction of those coastal towns must be seen to be believed.

7. Plagiarism is what one would call a _____ act.

8. The tyrant's plethora of _____ eventually led to his downfall.

9. The baseball game is running _____ the football game.

10. Claiming that your dog ate your homework is, without a doubt, a very _____ argument.

EXERCISE 36-C	Spelling Quiz – Track #11

Directions: √ Go to track #11 on CD #2.

√ For this quiz, you will hear a word, a phrase or an idiom. You will hear it twice. You will then have ten seconds to type it.

√ As you type the word(s), say each letter.

√ Check your answers in the word list on the previous page.

√ Record your score on page 201.

EXERCISE 36-D	60-Word Typing Test

Directions: You have 60 seconds to type the following passage. When you are finished, calculate your wpm score. Record your score on page 201.

Concurrent with the advent of the internet came the boom in online piracy. Simply put, online piracy is the wholesale theft of intellectual property. Those who advocate this brazen malefaction argue that it's a victimless crime. Such specious reasoning is emblematic of those whose parasitic chicanery is unrepentant. Unfortunately, these wayward souls ignore the adage: "What goes around comes around."

WPM Score =   **/ 60**

EXERCISE 37-A   Multiple-Choice Quiz

Directions: You have 2 minutes to complete this task. Do not use a dictionary. Check your answers on page 192. Record your score on page 201.

1. double-edged sword (id, n/adj)

a. when the outcome can be both positive and negative
b. when the outcome can be both certain and reliable
c. when the outcome is similar
d. when there is no clear outcome

2. organic (adj)

a. pure
b. natural
c. no chemicals
d. all of the above

3. produce (n)

a. fresh fruits and vegetables
b. basic ingredients
c. packaged goods
d. man-made comestibles

4. trendy (adj)

a. out of fashion
b. dated
c. in fashion
d. pragmatic

5. pesticide (n)

a. chemical to kill insects
b. chemical to kill bugs
c. chemical to kill pests
d. all of the above

6. cost an arm and a leg (id, v)

a. to be very expensive
b. to be extremely costly
c. to be not affordable
d. all of the above

7. take one's place in the spotlight (id, v)

a. to stand at the center of attention
b. to avoid any attention
c. to take attention away from one
d. to make money in movies

8. purport (v)

a. to deny
b. to claim
c. to bury
d. to import

9. nevertheless (adv)

a. yet
b. nonetheless
c. still
d. all of the above

10. unadulterated (adj)

a. touched
b. seasonal
c. changeable
d. untouched

EXERCISE 37-B   Sentence-Completion Quiz

<u>Directions</u>: You have 5 minutes to complete this task. Check your answers on page 192. Record your score on page 201.

<u>Word</u> <u>List</u>	double-edged sword • organic • produce • trendy • pesticide • cost an arm and a leg • take one's place in the spotlight • purport • nevertheless • unadulterated •

1. A Catch-22 is analogous to a _____ .

2. The _____ section at my grocery store has a wide variety of _____ produce.

3. It goes without saying that all herbicides and _____ are carcinogenic.

4. The government _____ that the recession is over.

5. The old bank closed and reopened as an _____ restaurant.

6. If you want to go to an Ivy League school, such as Yale, Harvard or Princeton, it will take a monumental effort. It will also _____ .

7. Zaheer likes to try out new restaurants, especially ones that are _____ .

8. With her new song, Shaka has finally _____ .

9. Graciela prefers to buy organic produce owing to the fact that she knows that it is _____ .

10. It was really snowing. _____ , Rene drove to work.

EXERCISE 37-C — Spelling Quiz – Track #12

Directions: √ Go to track #12 on CD #2.

√ For this quiz, you will hear a word, a phrase or an idiom. You will hear it twice. You will then have ten seconds to type it.

√ As you type the word(s), say each letter.

√ Check your answers in the word list on the previous page.

√ Record your score on page 201.

EXERCISE 37-D — 60-Word Typing Test

Directions: You have 60 seconds to type the following passage. When you are finished, calculate your wpm score. Record your score on page 201.

Organic food, once trendy, is finally taking its rightful place in the spotlight. Free of pesticides, herbicides and antibiotics, organic food purports to be food in its purest, most unadulterated form. However, organic produce can also be a double-edged sword: healthy, yes, but it can also cost an arm and a leg. Nevertheless, it's comforting to know what you're consuming.

WPM Score =   / 60

EXERCISE 38-A · Multiple-Choice Quiz

Directions: You have 2 minutes to complete this task. Do not use a dictionary. Check your answers on page 192. Record your score on page 201.

1. bite the bullet (id, v)

a. to do something unwillingly
b. to eat bullets for breakfast
c. to taste something terrible
d. to do something you love to do

2. anesthetic (n)

a. drug that wakes you up
b. drug that puts you to sleep
c. drug that makes you smile
d. drug that makes you forget

3. amputation (n)

a. cutting off limbs
b. increasing electricity
c. measuring the body
d. cutting off money

4. wounded (adj)

a. suffering bodily injury
b. physical damage
c. emotional damage
d. all of the above

5. evolved (adj)

a. transformed into
b. bought into
c. reduced into
d. dropped into

6. germ (n)

a. disease producing micro-organism
b. disease proof virus
c. disease killing micro-organism
d. unadulterated disease

7. surgery (n)

a. contractors repairing structures
b. friends healing wounds
c. presidents finding solutions
d. doctors cutting into the body

8. rampant (adj)

a. in control
b. automatic control
c. out of control
d. self-control

9. primitive (adj)

a. dated
b. old fashioned
c. lacking sophistication
d. all of the above

10. antiseptic (n/adj)

a. germ-killing solution
b. very clean
c. free of dirt and disease
d. all of the above

EXERCISE 38-B   Sentence-Completion Quiz

Directions: You have 5 minutes to complete this task. Check your answers on page 192. Record your score on page 201.

> Word
> List
>
> bite the bullet • anesthetic • amputation • wounded • evolved •
> germ • surgery • rampant • primitive • antiseptic •

1. Marica felt really _____ when her boyfriend forgot to buy her a birthday present.

2. Julie finally decided to _____ and register for the TOEFL test.

3. We should wash our hands whenever we can owing to the fact that _____ tend to accumulate there.

4. It's astounding how fast the personal computer has _____ just in the last few years.

5. Some believe that if we return to a more _____ state, we will be healthier and happier.

6. Jack is not keen on having _____ to repair his knees.

7. During the American Civil war, twenty-eight per cent of those soldiers who had an _____ died.

8. The governor purports that crime has decreased. However, the newspapers claim that crime is still _____ .

9. Listerine, perhaps the most famous mouthwash and _____ in the world today, is named after Joseph Lister, a seminal English scientist.

10. Tragically, Michael Jackson died from an overdose of a very powerful _____ .

EXERCISE 38-C — Spelling Quiz – Track #13

Directions: √ Go to track #13 on CD #2.

√ For this quiz, you will hear a word, a phrase or an idiom. You will hear it twice. You will then have ten seconds to type it.

√ As you type the word(s), say each letter.

√ Check your answers in the word list on the previous page.

√ Record your score on page 201.

EXERCISE 38-D — 60-Word Typing Test

Directions: You have 60 seconds to type the following passage. When you are finished, calculate your wpm score. Record your score on page 201.

Early battlefield hospitals were unimaginably primitive. Because there was no antiseptic, germs were rampant. Because there was no anesthetic, wounded soldiers were awake during surgery. The most common surgery was amputation. To prevent screaming, soldiers were given a bullet to bite, hence "Bite the bullet," an idiom that's evolved to mean forcing yourself to do something you don't want to.

WPM Score = _____ / 60

EXERCISE 39-A | Multiple-Choice Quiz

Directions: You have 2 minutes to complete this task. Do not use a dictionary. Check your answers on page 192. Record your score on page 201.

1. persnickety (adj)

a. fussy
b. strict
c. fastidious
d. all of the above

2. bent out of shape (adj)

a. really happy
b. really angry
c. really sad
d. really excited

3. sort (n)

a. address
b. brand
c. label
d. type

4. cross the Rubicon (id, v)

a. to cross the point of no return
b. to go too far
c. to cross a very big line
d. all of the above

5. Neanderthal (n/adj)

a. early cave man
b. lacking culture
c. brain-dead guy
d. all of the above

6. ascertain (v)

a. to discover with certainty
b. to learn with alarm
c. to learn with resolution
d. to learn nothing

7. transgression (n)

a. respect
b. violation
c. agreement
d. trans-national

8. multitude (n)

a. many
b. not much
c. some
d. all of the above

9. accumulate (v)

a. to intercept
b. to collect
c. to reject
d. to suspect

10. infringement (n)

a.   pressed into a small space
b.   measuring the space between two points
c.   being too far away
d.   too close without permission

| EXERCISE 39-B | Sentence-Completion Quiz |

Directions: You have 5 minutes to complete this task. Check your answers on page 192. Record your score on page 201.

| <u>Word List</u> | persnickety • bent out of shape • sort • cross the Rubicon • Neanderthal • ascertain • transgression • multitude • accumulate • infringement • |

1. Pedro's grandmother is so _____ . Whenever the family eats at her place, everyone has to sit in the exact same spot as the time before.

2. The professor got really _____ when he discovered that one of his students had plagiarized his latest research.

3. Scientists have _____ that there is water on the Moon.

4. Barton is what I would call the enigmatic _____ .

5. A series of patent _____ by a competitor forced Apple to sue for protection.

6. When you look up into the cosmos at night, you will see a _____ of stars.

7. Living on the frontier, cowboys had to _____ a lot of experience quickly if they wanted to survive.

8. The idiom "cross the Rubicon" originates in the Roman era when Julius Caesar was faced with a Catch-22: "Do I," Caesar wondered, "cross the Rubicon River and enter Rome with my victorious army (which was wholly illegal at the time) or do I remain an obedient soldier and keep my army beyond the Rubicon, and never return to the city that I love?" In the end, Caesar _____ .

9. If you ask me, she married a _____ .

10. Cheating on a final exam is, without a doubt, a major academic _____ .

EXERCISE 39-C — Spelling Quiz – Track #14

Directions: √ Go to track #14 on CD #2.

√ For this quiz, you will hear a word, a phrase or an idiom. You will hear it twice. You will then have ten seconds to type it.

√ As you type the word(s), say each letter.

√ Check your answers in the word list on the previous page.

√ Record your score on page 201.

EXERCISE 39-D — 60-Word Typing Test

Directions: You have 60 seconds to type the following passage. When you are finished, calculate your wpm score. Record your score on page 201.

Horace, a persnickety sort, got bent out of shape one day when he ascertained that his neighbor, a Neanderthal named Pete, had put up a fence that overshot the property line by a wide margin. It wasn't Pete's first transgression. No. As an inveterate trespasser, he had accumulated a multitude of minor infringements. But this time he'd crossed the Rubicon.

WPM Score =   **/ 60**

EXERCISE 40-A | Multiple-Choice Quiz

<u>Directions</u>: You have 2 minutes to complete this task. Do not use a dictionary. Check your answers on page 192. Record your score on page 201.

1. mosquito (n)

a. two-winged insect that sucks blood
b. four-winged insect that sucks blood
c. six-winged insect that sucks blood
d. all of the above

2. virus (n)

a. dangerous code that destroys PCs
b. sub-microscopic parasite that causes disease
c. pathogen
d. all of the above

3. tropical (adj)

a. land with lots of sun and rain
b. land in the equatorial zones
c. land that is arid and arable
d. lands that are hot and humid

4. ensure (v)

a. to make safe
b. to make secure
c. to protect
d. all of the above

5. nausea (n)

a. feeling an ache in the head
b. bone pain
c. sick feeling in the stomach
d. feeling discombobulated

6. incubation (n)

a. period of no growth
b. period of cold-induced growth
c. moment of realization
d. period of heat-induced growth

7. fever (n)

a. high body temperature
b. low body temperature
c. normal body temperature
d. decreasing body temperature

8. toxic (adj)

a. poisonous
b. harmful
c. deadly
d. all of the above

9. jaundiced (adj)

a. skeptical
b. cynical
c. skin having turned yellow
d. all of the above

10. immunity (n)

a. protection
b. free from
c. under no obligation
d. all of the above

EXERCISE 40-B   Sentence-Completion Quiz

Directions: You have 5 minutes to complete this task. Check your answers on page 192. Record your score on page 201.

Word List	mosquito • virus • tropical • ensure • nausea • incubation • fever • toxic • jaundiced • immunity •

1. The witness requested _____ from prosecution before he would agree to testify.

2. When Joanne went for a cruise on her honeymoon, she got really seasick and suffered from _____ .

3. A manifestation of influenza is a high _____ .

4. _____ breed profusely in stagnant water.

5. There are a myriad of _____ diseases for which there are no known vaccines.

6. A flu vaccine does not _____ immunity.

7. The residents near that polluting factory are living in a _____ environment.

8. Henri is such a cynic. His view of the world is so _____ , he doesn't trust anyone anymore.

9. Ironically, hackers who create dangerous computer _____ are often hired by big companies to write security software to protect against future virus attacks.

10. The _____ period for a chicken egg is about twenty-one days.

EXERCISE 40-C   Spelling Quiz – Track #15

Directions: √ Go to track #15 on CD #2.

√ For this quiz, you will hear a word, a phrase or an idiom. You will hear it twice. You will then have ten seconds to type it.

√ As you type the word(s), say each letter.

√ Check your answers in the word list on the previous page.

√ Record your score on page 201.

EXERCISE 40-D   60-Word Typing Test

Directions: You have 60 seconds to type the following passage. When you are finished, calculate your wpm score. Record your score on page 201.

Yellow fever, a virus transmitted by mosquitoes, is an infectious disease found in the tropical and sub-tropical zones of Africa and South America. After an incubation period of three to six days, symptoms are nausea, fever and pain. In 25% of cases, a toxic phase occurs causing liver damage which precipitates jaundice. Surviving yellow fever ensures a life-long immunity.

WPM Score =   / 60

Review #8

Directions: You have 60 seconds to complete this task. Do not use a dictionary. Check your answers on page 192. Record your score on page 201.

1. advent of (phr)

a. the introduction of
b. the development of
c. the invention of
d. all of the above

2. nevertheless (adv)

a. yet
b. nonetheless
c. still
d. all of the above

3. germ (n)

a. disease producing micro-organism
b. disease proof virus
c. disease killing micro-organism
d. disease spreading virus

4. ascertain (v)

a. to discover with certainty
b. to learn with alarm
c. to learn with resolution
d. to learn nothing

5. Neanderthal (n/adj)

a. early cave man
b. lacking culture
c. brain-dead guy
d. all of the above

6. tropical (adj)

a. land with lots of sun and rain
b. land that is arid and arable
c. lands that are hot and humid
d. land in the equatorial zones

7. immunity (n)

a. protection
b. free from
c. under no obligation
d. all of the above

8. bite the bullet (id, v)

a. to do something unwillingly
b. to eat bullets for breakfast
c. to taste something terrible
d. to do something you love to do

9. purport (v)

a. to deny
b. to claim
c. to bury
d. to import

10. parasitic (adj)

a. benefiting by working with another
b. benefiting from another's hard work
c. benefiting with no effort
d. all of the above

EXERCISE 41-A Multiple-Choice Quiz

Directions: You have 2 minutes to complete this task. Do not use a dictionary. Check your answers on page 192. Record your score on page 201.

1. feral (adj)

a. indigenous
b. wild
c. domestic
d. tame

2. prodigious (adj)

a. extraordinary
b. below average
c. small
d. predictable

3. deem (v)

a. to dream
b. to judge
c. to overwhelm
d. to ratify

4. invasive (adj)

a. one that destroys
b. one that confounds
c. one that invades
d. one that resides

5. cross (v)

a. to breed two different species
b. to cross fertilize
c. to interbreed
d. all of the above

6. hybrid (adj)

a. result of cross-breeding
b. mixture
c. amalgam
d. all of the above

7. propensity (n)

a. tendency
b. need
c. ability
d. all of the above

8. litter (n)

a. shimmering light
b. form of measurement
c. short message in writing
d. group of new born animals

9. sustenance (n)

a. food
b. nourishment
c. comestibles
d. all of the above

10. harbor (v)

a. to have
b. to possess
c. to hold
d. all of the above

EXERCISE 41-B   Sentence-Completion Quiz

Directions: You have 5 minutes to complete this task. Check your answers on page 192. Record your score on page 201.

> | Word List | feral • prodigious • deem • invasive • cross • hybrid • litter propensity • sustenance • harbor • |
> | --- | --- |

1. Even though zoo animals are kept in cages or in enclosures, they are still _____ .

2. Karen's dog just had a _____ of eight puppies.

3. Many _____ species of plant have taken root in America, none more so than the kudzu.

4. Apex predators have a _____ to be transient inasmuch as they need to travel to find enough _____ .

5. Phyllis is very much the type to buy a _____ car.

6. With the advent of agriculture, people could depend less on hunting for their _____ .

7. The doctor has _____ it necessary for Brice to have surgery.

8. The goldadoodle, a very trendy dog, is a _____ between a golden retriever and a poodle.

9. Some anthropologists postulate that Neanderthals became extinct because they were not _____ breeders.

10. When Julius Caesar crossed the Rubicon, he _____ no illusions about what might be waiting for him in Rome since bringing an army into Rome was a major transgression of Roman law.

EXERCISE 41-C | Spelling Quiz – Track #16

Directions: √ Go to track #16 on CD #2.

√ For this quiz, you will hear a word, a phrase or an idiom. You will hear it twice. You will then have ten seconds to type it.

√ As you type the word(s), say each letter.

√ Check your answers in the word list on the previous page.

√ Record your score on page 201.

EXERCISE 41-D | 60-Word Typing Test

Directions: You have 60 seconds to type the following passage. When you are finished, calculate your wpm score. Record your score on page 201.

Years ago, domestic American pigs were crossed with wild Russian boars. The result was the feral hog, a pig hybrid that harbors no fear of man. Feral hogs are deemed an invasive species due to their propensity to destroy habitat while searching for sustenance, and for their prodigious breeding. A sow can produce a litter of eight piglets twice yearly.

WPM Score = / 60

EXERCISE 42-A | Multiple-Choice Quiz

Directions: You have 2 minutes to complete this task. Do not use a dictionary. Check your answers on page 192. Record your score on page 201.

1. element (n)

a. fundamental substance
b. distinct form
c. having one kind of atom
d. all of the above

2. respiration (n)

a. act of breathing
b. act of perspiring
c. act of regeneration
d. act of retiring

3. decay (v)

a. to break down
b. to fall apart
c. to disintegrate
d. all of the above

4. combust (v)

a. to burn
b. to yearn
c. to spurn
d. to learn

5. evaporate (v)

a. to breath slowly
b. to exchange money
c. to change into paper
d. to convert into a vapor

6. biosphere (n)

a. area of world where life exists
b. area of famine and drought
c. area of greatest learning
d. area where life existed

7. pedosphere (n)

a. area of world with dirt
b. area of world with soil
c. area of world with earth
d. all of the above

8. geosphere (n)

a. rock-based part of the world
b. that studied by geologists
c. solid parts of the earth
d. all of the above

9. hydrosphere (n)

a. all the water found on earth
b. water container
c. place water goes
d. process of changing salt water into fresh water

10. eruption (n)

a. quiet conversion
b. violent explosion
c. regular movement
d. minimal change

EXERCISE 42-B   Sentence-Completion Quiz

Directions: You have 5 minutes to complete this task. Check your answers on page 192. Record your score on page 201.

<u>Word</u> <u>List</u>	element • respiration • decay • combust • evaporate • pedosphere • geosphere • hydrosphere • biosphere • eruptions •

1. Water is composed of two _____ : hydrogen and oxygen.

2. If you leave a cup of water in a desert, it will quickly _____ .

3. The water cycle, in which water is evaporated and returns to the earth as precipitation, takes place in the _____ .

4. If you drop a burning match into gasoline, the gasoline will, without a doubt, _____ .

5. With the advent of the mass production of refined sugar in Britain in the mid-eighteenth century came the problem of rampant tooth _____ .

6. Geologists are primarily concerned with events happening in the _____ .

7. If you are a soil scientist, your primary field of study is the _____ .

8. The _____ of Mount Saint Helens, truly a cataclysmic event, caused devastating earthquakes and avalanches.

9. _____ is not an integral part of photosynthesis.

10. The word _____ was coined by geologist Eduard Suess in 1875.

EXERCISE 42-C   Spelling Quiz – Track #17

Directions: √ Go to track #17 on CD #2.

√ For this quiz, you will hear a word, a phrase or an idiom. You will hear it twice. You will then have ten seconds to type it.

√ As you type the word(s), say each letter.

√ Check your answers in the word list on the previous page.

√ Record your score on page 201.

EXERCISE 42-D   60-Word Typing Test

Directions: You have 60 seconds to type the following passage. When you are finished, calculate your wpm score. Record your score on page 201.

Carbon (C), the most important element on earth, is released into the atmosphere a myriad of ways: plant and animal respiration, decaying plant and animal matter, fossil fuel combustion, cement production, ocean water evaporation, and volcanic eruption. Carbon is then recycled between the biosphere, the pedosphere, the geosphere, and the hydrosphere. Scientists call this complex carbon exchange the biogeochemical cycle.

WPM Score =   / 60

EXERCISE 43-A Multiple-Choice Quiz

Directions: You have 2 minutes to complete this task. Do not use a dictionary. Check your answers on page 192. Record your score on page 201.

1. post war (adj)

a. period after a war
b. period before a war
c. period during a war
d. prosperity after a war

2. case in point (phr)

a. for example
b. specifically
c. namely
d. all of the above

3. passion (n)

a. love for
b. hate for
c. need for
d. wish for

4. culinary (adj)

a. related with kitchens
b. related with food
c. related with cooking
d. all of the above

5. accomplished (adj)

a. failed
b. successful
c. average
d. marginal

6. chef (n)

a. boss of a store
b. boss of a kitchen
c. boss of a police department
d. head Indian

7. chagrin (n)

a. realization
b. joy
c. anger
d. disappointment

8. despise (v)

a. to love
b. to cherish
c. to hate
d. to accept

9. ground-breaking (adj)

a. revolutionary
b. seminal
c. original
d. all of the above

10. gourmand (n)

a.   lover of gourds
b.   lover of poetry
c.   lover of food
d.   lover of cars

EXERCISE 43-B   Sentence-Completion Quiz

Directions: You have 5 minutes to complete this task. Check your answers on page 192. Record your score on page 201.

Word List	post war • case in point • passion • culinary • accomplished • chef • chagrin • despise • ground-breaking • gourmand •

1. Rock and roll had its genesis in _____ World _____ Two America while jazz had its genesis in _____ World _____ One America.

2. If a professional _____ wants to be successful, he or she must keep their nose to the grindstone.

3. Chef Charles has a _____ for creating vegan dishes.

4. Bill and his wife Dolorous, with their passion for food and wine, are what one would call _____ .

5. With the advent of _____ schools, there has been a boom in organic restaurants.

6. Alex _____ fast food. He prefers his food to be unadulterated.

7. Much to Raquel's _____ , her favorite restaurant went bankrupt.

8. Orcas are _____ killers.

9. Many inventions are the result of an accident. _____ : the microwave oven. Microwaves were originally developed for use in radar. Only by accident did scientists discover that microwaves also cooked food.

10. It goes without saying that Darwin's theory of evolution was a _____ idea.

EXERCISE 43-C — Spelling Quiz – Track #18

Directions: √ Go to track #18 on CD #2.

√ For this quiz, you will hear a word, a phrase or an idiom. You will hear it twice. You will then have ten seconds to type it.

√ As you type the word(s), say each letter.

√ Check your answers in the word list on the previous page.

√ Record your score on page 201.

EXERCISE 43-D — 60-Word Typing Test

Directions: You have 60 seconds to type the following passage. When you are finished, calculate your wpm score. Record your score on page 201.

Not all revolutions are political. Some are culinary. Case in point: Julia Child. While living in post war Paris, she developed a passion for cooking and became an accomplished chef. Yet, much to her chagrin, the average American housewife despised cooking. Julia changed all that. Her ground-breaking cook book liberated women from canned food and inspired a new generation of gourmands.

WPM Score = _____ / 60

EXERCISE 44-A   Multiple-Choice Quiz

Directions: You have 2 minutes to complete this task. Do not use a dictionary. Check your answers on page 192. Record your score on page 201.

1. obtuse (adj)

a. stupid
b. brilliant
c. average
d. different

2. conundrum (n)

a. challenging problem
b. problem with no obvious answer
c. puzzlement
d. all of the above

3. diffidence (n)

a. lots of confidence
b. no confidence
c. growing confidence
d. all of the above

4. albeit (adv)

a. but
b. although
c. though
d. all of the above

5. inscrutable (adj)

a. comprehensible
b. impenetrable
c. territorial
d. horrible

6. insurmountable (adj)

a. impossible
b. cannot be conquered
c. unresolvable
d. all of the above

7. countenance (n)

a. expression on one's face
b. feeling in one's heart
c. idea in one's head
d. money in one's wallet

8. ebullient (adj)

a. always rancorous
b. always enthusiastic
c. always perplexed
d. always bored

9. disconcerted (adj)

a. perplexed
b. discombobulated
c. embarrassed
d. all of the above

10. nail (id, v)

a. to answer correctly
b. to attain a goal
c. to target and hit
d. all of the above

EXERCISE 44-B — Sentence-Completion Quiz

Directions: You have 5 minutes to complete this task. Check your answers on page 192. Record your score on page 201.

<u>Word</u>
<u>List</u>   obtuse • conundrum • diffidence • albeit • inscrutable • nail •
            countenance • ebullient • disconcerted • insurmountable •

1. Norman's _____ suggested that he was not yet ready to sign the contract.

2. Willy always asks such _____ questions. Case in point: "Is there really cheese on the Moon?"

3. Whenever Hank visits the dentist, he always feels so _____ .

4. Ferdinand's team, in last place, lost to the first place team _____ by only one point.

5. Trudy is always so _____ . She is always ready to do anything or go anywhere.

6. In law class, Charles _____ the breach-of-contract question.

7. The judge's countenance was _____ . He gave nothing away.

8. The teacher asked Johnnie if he'd done his homework. The _____ look on Johnnie's face said it all.

9. For many test-takers, the TOEFL test seems _____ . Yet, with practice they soon realize that it is not entirely _____ .

10. A Catch-22 is definitely a _____ .

EXERCISE 44-C Spelling Quiz – Track #19

Directions: √ Go to track #19 on CD #2.

√ For this quiz, you will hear a word, a phrase or an idiom. You will hear it twice. You will then have ten seconds to type it.

√ As you type the word(s), say each letter.

√ Check your answers in the word list on the previous page.

√ Record your score on page 201.

EXERCISE 44-D 60-Word Typing Test

Directions: You have 60 seconds to type the following passage. When you are finished, calculate your wpm score. Record your score on page 201.

Erica was feeling totally obtuse because the conundrum their math teacher had given them was so inscrutable it seemed impossible to solve. Melissa, her countenance manifesting diffidence, glanced at her best friend Melissa. Ever ebullient Melissa was a brainiac albeit even she was looking disconcerted over the insurmountable problem before her. Not Kevin. The nerd had totally nailed the problem.

WPM Score =   / 60

EXERCISE 45-A   Multiple-Choice Quiz

Directions: You have 2 minutes to complete this task. Do not use a dictionary. Check your answers on page 192. Record your score on page 201.

1. infamous (adj)

a. famous for a good reputation
b. famous for a bad reputation
c. having a famous name
d. having no name

2. entrepreneur (n)

a. French for assiduous worker
b. French for underachiever
c. French for independent business person
d. German for between friends

3. take no prisoners (id, v)

a. to show no pity
b. to show no compassion
c. to show no weakness
d. all of the above

4. all manner of (adj)

a. all kinds of
b. great variety of
c. myriad of
d. all of the above

5. widget (n)

a. name of a successful product
b. name of a foreign product
c. name of a failing product
d. name of a non specific product or contrivance

6. peddle (v)

a. to buy
b. to keep
c. to sell
d. to invest

7. budding (adj)

a. young and learning
b. young and wayward
c. young and fast
d. young and lazy

8. expand one's horizons (id, v)

a. to invade a country
b. to explore new territory
c. to invest in a country
d. to stay close to home

9. rake in (id, v)

a. to make a lot of transgressions
b. to make a lot hybrids
c. to make a lot of money
d. to make a lot of friends

10. resurrect (v)

a. to bring back from the dead
b. to give new life
c. to make new again
d. all of the above

EXERCISE 45-B | Sentence-Completion Quiz

Directions: You have 5 minutes to complete this task. Check your answers on page 192. Record your score on page 201.

Word List	infamous • entrepreneur • take no prisoners • all manner of • widget • peddle • budding • expand one's horizons • rake in • resurrect •

1. If you were an _____ , the American frontier was a good place to try and make a buck.

2. Sylvia loves to collect _____ of old dolls.

3. The rapper J-Boy is _____ for a multitude of transgressions.

4. Katerina wants to _____ by studying in America for a year.

5. Madhur is a _____ painter with a passion for landscapes.

6. Pedro's plans are black and white. He wants to climb the corporate ladder and _____ a big salary.

7. Jutiporn is the captain of her own ship. If someone breaks a contract with her company, she tells her lawyers to sue and "_____ ."

8. If Hong Bo wants his new product to be successful worldwide, he must get out there and really _____ it.

9. If you can't dream up a name for your new mechanical invention, simply call it a _____ for the time being.

10. Many want to _____ the old colonial law that says you can't buy alcohol on Sunday.

EXERCISE 45-C | Spelling Quiz – Track #20

<u>Directions</u>: √ Go to track #20 on CD #2.

√ For this quiz, you will hear a word, a phrase or an idiom. You will hear it twice. You will then have ten seconds to type it.

√ As you type the word(s), say each letter.

√ Check your answers in the word list on the previous page.

√ Record your score on page 201.

EXERCISE 45-D | 60-Word Typing Test

<u>Directions</u>: You have 60 seconds to type the following passage. When you are finished, calculate your wpm score. Record your score on page 201.

As a budding entrepreneur, Josef made his mark peddling all manner of contrivances. Wanting to expand his horizons, he rolled the dice and invested all his money in a failing widget factory. In no time, he'd resurrected the factory and was raking it in. Josef is now infamous for taking no prisoners when setting the price for his personal computers.

WPM Score = / 60

Review #9

Directions: You have 60 seconds to complete this task. Do not use a dictionary. Check your answers on page 192. Record your score on page 201.

1. deem (v)

a. to dream
b. to judge
c. to overwhelm
d. to ratify

2. decay (v)

a. to break down
b. to fall apart
c. to disintegrate
d. all of the above

3. ground-breaking (adj)

a. revolutionary
b. seminal
c. original
d. all of the above

4. conundrum (n)

a. challenging problem
b. problem with no obvious answer
c. puzzlement
d. all of the above

5. entrepreneur (n)

a. French for assiduous worker
b. French for underachiever
c. French for independent business person
d. German for between friends

6. hybrid (adj)

a. result of cross-breeding
b. mixture
c. amalgam
d. all of the above

7. hydrosphere (n)

a. all the water found on earth
b. water container
c. place water goes
d. process of changing salt water into fresh water

8. accomplished (adj)

a. failed
b. successful
c. average
d. marginal

9. inscrutable (adj)

a. comprehensible
b. impenetrable
c. territorial
d. horrible

10. infamous (adj)

a. famous for a good reputation
b. famous for a bad reputation
c. having a famous name
d. having no name

EXERCISE 46-A　Multiple-Choice Quiz

<u>**Directions:**</u> You have 2 minutes to complete this task. Do not use a dictionary. Check your answers on page 192. Record your score on page 201.

1. employ (v)

a. to use
b. to reject
c. to herd
d. to take root

2. datum (n)

a. singular form of date
b. part of something smaller
c. singular form of data
d. all of the above

3. bacteria (n)

a. plural of back
b. plural of bachelor
c. plural of Bactrian
d. plural of bacterium

4. criteria (n)

a. list of rules used to judge
b. plural of criterion
c. points to follow when evaluating
d. all of the above

5. memoranda (n)

a. memos
b. plural of memorandum
c. a myriad of messages
d. all of the above

6. stigmata (n)

a. lines
b. dots
c. marks
d. squares

7. peruse (v)

a. to examine carefully
b. to prepare properly
c. to prescribe carefully
d. to provide often

8. deal with (v)

a. to take care of
b. to take action
c. to confront
d. all of the above

9. salient (adj)

a. one that rises above the rest
b. one lower than all the rest
c. one equal to all the rest
d. one harder than all the rest

10. as in (phr)

a. for example
b. such as
c. namely
d. all of the above

EXERCISE 46-B   Sentence-Completion Quiz

Directions: You have 5 minutes to complete this task. Check your answers on page 192. Record your score on page 201.

Word List	employ • datum • bacteria • criteria • memoranda • stigmata • peruse • deal with • salient • as in •

1. By _____ robots, the company was able to reduce its labor costs substantially.

2. _____ is synonymous with cuts or wounds.

3. Arguably, that particular piece of _____ is not accurate.

4. _____ are an integral part of the decaying process.

5. Sofia loves to _____ the shops on Fifth Avenue.

6. Roland _____ his problems by taking the bull by the horns.

7. Every Monday, Lee's boss sends out a plethora of _____ reminding everyone to keep their noses to the grindstone.

8. Part of M.I.T.'s admission _____ for foreign students is a high TOEFL score.

9. At the end of the lecture, the professor restated the most _____ point.

10. Starving is synonymous with ravenous, _____ ,"After Katie works out, she is ravenous."

EXERCISE 46-C | Spelling Quiz – Track #21

Directions: √ Go to track #21 on CD #2.

√ For this quiz, you will hear a word, a phrase or an idiom. You will hear it twice. You will then have ten seconds to type it.

√ As you type the word(s), say each letter.

√ Check your answers in the word list on the previous page.

√ Record your score on page 201.

EXERCISE 46-D | 60-Word Typing Test

Directions: You have 60 seconds to type the following passage. When you are finished, calculate your wpm score. Record your score on page 201.

In the reading section, TOEFL often employs plural words ending in "a", such as media and its singular, medium. Let's peruse a few more salient examples: stigmata and stigmatum; bacteria and bacterium; criteria and criterion; memoranda and memorandum; data and datum, as in "The data in the memorandum dealt with the criteria for measuring the stigmata left by the bacterium."

WPM Score =   / 60

EXERCISE 47-A   Multiple-Choice Quiz

Directions: You have 2 minutes to complete this task. Do not use a dictionary. Check your answers on page 192. Record your score on page 201.

1. mince words (v)

a. to be uncertain
b. to render incomplete
c. to soften one's words
d. all of the above

2. epiphany (n)

a. innate moment of realization
b. sudden revelation
c. personal discovery
d. all of the above

3. boon (n)

a. pain
b. loss
c. benefit
d. disadvantage

4. ersatz (adj)

a. German word for fake
b. knock off
c. forgery
d. all of the above

5. disingenuous (adj)

a. sincere
b. honest
c. insincere
d. kind

6. endemic (adj)

a. catching
b. contagious
c. spreading
d. all of the above

7. expediency (n)

a. palette
b. code
c. convenience
d. affordability

8. bevy of (phr)

a. a myriad of
b. many
c. a lot of
d. all of the above

9. hand in (v)

a. to submit
b. to remit
c. to prohibit
d. to elicit

10. expunge (v)

a.   to include completely
b.   to delete totally
c.   to enter often
d.   to record carefully

EXERCISE 47-B   Sentence-Completion Quiz

<u>Directions</u>: You have 5 minutes to complete this task. Check your answers on page 192. Record your score on page 201.

<u>Word</u> <u>List</u>	mince words • epiphany • ersatz • boon • disingenuous • endemic • expunge • hand in • bevy of • expediency •

1. At the end of class, the students had to _____ their essays.

2. The usually ebullient prime minister did not _____ when she said that she would increase the corporate tax substantially.

3. On Canal Street in Manhattan, you can peruse many small shops that sell _____ designer hand bags.

4. Lower fuel costs are a definite _____ for all.

5. When Carlos got a perfect 5 on his TOEFL independent essay, he had an _____ . He realized that getting a perfect essay score was not insurmountable after all.

6. It goes without saying that the president's plan to reduce the income tax rate will make many voters happy. However, the plan is simply political _____ . In the short term, it will win the president some votes, but it will not solve the long term problem of reducing the national debt.

7. A computer virus can easily _____ all the information on your hard drive.

8. Jacob's boss said everyone at the company would get a ten percent raise. That was six months ago, and still no raise. Talk about _____ .

9. Tomas has a _____ TOEFL books.

10. Smoking among pre-teens is _____ .

EXERCISE 47-C Spelling Quiz – Track #22

Directions: √ Go to track #22 on CD #2.

√ For this quiz, you will hear a word, a phrase or an idiom. You will hear it twice. You will then have ten seconds to type it.

√ As you type the word(s), say each letter.

√ Check your answers in the word list on the previous page.

√ Record your score on page 201.

EXERCISE 47-D 60-Word Typing Test

Directions: You have 60 seconds to type the following passage. When you are finished, calculate your wpm score. Record your score on page 201.

The professor didn't mince words. "I've had an epiphany," he told his class. "Plagiarism is endemic. Truly, the expediency of the web is a boon for researchers yet it has left a bevy of ersatz essays on my desk. Handing in a plagiarized essay is not only disingenuous but will also get you kicked out and your academic record expunged."

WPM Score =   / 60

EXERCISE 48-A | Multiple-Choice Quiz

Directions: You have 2 minutes to complete this task. Do not use a dictionary. Check your answers on page 192. Record your score on page 201.

1. zenith (n)

a. highest point
b. opposite of nadir
c. the absolute top
d. all of the above

2. laissez-faire (phr)

a. closed-market business approach
b. free-market business model
c. foreign-market business style
d. all of the above

3. impugn (v)

a. to agree
b. to attack
c. to borrow
d. to incubate

4. epitome (n)

a. quality
b. quintessence
c. epistle
d. underachiever

5. equanimity (n)

a. anger
b. pride
c. equality
d. calm

6. placate (v)

a. to assuage
b. to mollify
c. to pacify
d. all of the above

7. resplendent (adj)

a. brilliant and amazing
b. educational and important
c. boring and ridiculous
d. silly and persnickety

8. impervious (adj)

a. vulnerable to attack
b. ready to attack
c. invulnerable to attack
d. always under attack

9. harangue (n/v)

a. short, fun lecture
b. short, dull lecture
c. long, angry lecture
d. academic lecture

10. rancor (n)

a. joy
b. anger
c. fear
d. all of the above

EXERCISE 48-B   Sentence-Completion Quiz

Directions: You have 5 minutes to complete this task. Check your answers on page 192. Record your score on page 201.

Word List	zenith • impugn • laissez-faire • epitome • equanimity • placate • rancor • harangue • impervious • resplendent •

1. The dot.com bubble reached its _____ on March 10, 2000 when the stock market hit a new high.

2. Many in England argue that royalty is superfluous. On the contrary, many believe that there is nothing more emblematic of England than their benevolent Queen _____ in her crown.

3. _____ the president is an integral part of the American political process.

4. LeMichael is wary of his parents because whenever they talk, they always _____ him about getting a job.

5. Sir Isaac Newton, the esteemed eighteenth century British scientist who created calculus and the theory of gravity, among other seminal achievements, is the _____ of genius.

6. Is the Earth _____ to black holes? That is the $64,000.00 question.

7. It's hard for Al to think of his future with any degree of _____ , especially when his boss just pulled the plug on his research.

8. When the drought was at its _____ , the tyrannical Queen tried to _____ her people by enumerating the harbingers of rain she'd seen.

9. In the 1970s, the Chicago School of Economics championed a _____ system of business in South and Central America, a brand of free-market capitalism which was, without a doubt, an overwhelming failure.

10. _____ precipitates stress.

EXERCISE 48-C	Spelling Quiz – Track #23

Directions: √ Go to track #23 on CD #2.

    √ For this quiz, you will hear a word, a phrase or an idiom. You will hear it twice. You will then have ten seconds to type it.

    √ As you type the word(s), say each letter.

    √ Check your answers in the word list on the previous page.

    √ Record your score on page 201.

EXERCISE 48-D	60-Word Typing Test

Directions: You have 60 seconds to type the following passage. When you are finished, calculate your wpm score. Record your score on page 201.

The president was at his zenith when critics started to impugn his laissez-faire approach to business. The president, the epitome of equanimity, tried to placate his detractors by having a succession of resplendent dinners at the White House. Yet the rancor of his foes went unappeased. The president, impervious to the harangues of his critics, simply refused to play ball.

WPM Score =   / 60

EXERCISE 49-A   Multiple-Choice Quiz

Directions: You have 2 minutes to complete this task. Do not use a dictionary. Check your answers on page 192. Record your score on page 201.

1. adaptable (adj)

a. able to demonstrate
b. able to adjust
c. able to construct
d. all of the above

2. voracious (adj)

a. never hungry
b. rarely hungry
c. always hungry
d. always in a hurry

3. testosterone (n)

a. male hormone
b. female virus
c. pathogen for omnivores
d. female hormone

4. murky (adj)

a. clear
b. thin
c. not clear
d. thick

5. target (v)

a. to kill
b. to invade
c. to focus on
d. to symbolize

6. territorial (adj)

a. searching for new land
b. traveling in new territory
c. protective of one's land
d. wanting to buy more land

7. fatality (n)

a. death
b. loss
c. casualty
d. all of the above

8. unpredictable (adj)

a. cannot be rendered
b. cannot be predicted
c. cannot be evaluated
d. cannot be expected

9. patrol (v)

a. to defend an area totally
b. to check and recheck an area
c. to fight and die for a cause
d. to sink or swim for no reason

10. attribute to (v)

a.   to give credit to
b.   to acknowledge
c.   to give benefit to
d.   all of the above

EXERCISE 49-B   Sentence-Completion Quiz

Directions: You have 5 minutes to complete this task. Check your answers on page 192. Record your score on page 201.

<u>Word</u> <u>List</u>	adaptable • voracious • testosterone • murky • target • patrol • territorial • fatality • unpredictable • attribute to •

1. It is difficult for a predator to _____ its prey if the prey is well camouflaged.

2. Male lions _____ their territory assiduously.

3. A mother bird must constantly feed her _____ brood of chicks.

4. Those who live Spartanly are usually very _____ .

5. Catfish are right at home in _____ water.

6. It is difficult to _____ the invention of the internet _____ just one person.

7. The behavior of the rock star was wholly _____ .

8. Most professional athletes eschew _____ as a means of improving performance.

9. Whenever we push the envelope in space, there will always be _____ .

10. As a take-no-prisoners salesman, Charlie is highly _____ .

EXERCISE 49-C Spelling Quiz – Track #24

Directions: √ Go to track #24 on CD #2.

√ For this quiz, you will hear a word, a phrase or an idiom. You will hear it twice. You will then have ten seconds to type it.

√ As you type the word(s), say each letter.

√ Check your answers in the word list on the previous page.

√ Record your score on page 201.

EXERCISE 49-D 60-Word Typing Test

Directions: You have 60 seconds to type the following passage. When you are finished, calculate your wpm score. Record your score on page 201.

The bull shark is highly adaptable, surviving in both fresh and salt water. In addition, its voracious appetite targets anything that moves. Because it patrols shallow, murky water, the majority of human fatalities are attributed to the bull shark. They are territorial, unpredictable, and extremely aggressive owing to their inordinate level of testosterone, the highest of any animal, even tigers.

WPM Score =   / 60

EXERCISE 50-A | Multiple-Choice Quiz

<u>Directions</u>: You have 2 minutes to complete this task. Do not use a dictionary. Check your answers on page 192. Record your score on page 201.

1. clear the air about (id, v)

a. to eliminate any ambiguity
b. to set right
c. to make clear once and for all
d. all of the above

2. invention (n)

a. traditional idea
b. original idea
c. believable idea
d. all of the above

3. excise (v)

a. to exercise
b. to exacerbate
c. to delete
d. to ameliorate

4. excluding (adj)

a. act of bringing in
b. act of keeping in
c. act of keeping out
d. act of looking excellent

5. code (n)

a. form of arcane communication
b. invented language
c. language using symbols
d. all of the above

6. vernacular (n)

a. mainstream language
b. native tongue
c. indigenous language
d. all of the above

7. jargon (n)

a. form of slang
b. inclusive not exclusive code
c. code for special applications
d. all of the above

8. aficionado (n)

a. official
b. fan
c. friend
d. developer

9. grasp (v)

a. to complete
b. to understand
c. to believe
d. to render

10. gang (n)

a. group with a common identity
b. group with its own verbal code
c. anti-social group with a hierarchy
d. all of the above

EXERCISE 50-B   Sentence-Completion Quiz

Directions: You have 5 minutes to complete this task. Check your answers on page 192. Record your score on page 201.

Word List	clear the air about • invention • excise • excluding • code • jargon • vernacular • aficionado • grasp • gang •

1. Alina is a poetry _____ .

2. Mouse, hard drive and memory are examples of computer _____ .

3. Abra had no difficulty _____ the most salient point in the meeting.

4. _____ _____ English is a challenge for many non native speakers inasmuch as it has a plethora of idioms, jargon and slang.

5. Many famous rappers were, and still are, _____ members.

6. Gangs employ slang, a form of verbal _____ that non gang members, such as the police (and parents), cannot grasp.

7. What is the greatest _____ ever? That is the $64,000.00 question.

8. The president will meet the press to _____ about why he decided to send more troops abroad.

9. Some countries have _____ infamous parts of their histories from school text books.

10. Slang is an _____ _____ designed to be grasped only by those within the gang.

EXERCISE 50-C	Spelling Quiz – Track #25

Directions: √ Go to track #25 on CD #2.

√ For this quiz, you will hear a word, a phrase or an idiom. You will hear it twice. You will then have ten seconds to type it.

√ As you type the word(s), say each letter.

√ Check your answers in the word list on the previous page.

√ Record your score on page 201.

EXERCISE 50-D	60-Word Typing Test

Directions: You have 60 seconds to type the following passage. When you are finished, calculate your wpm score. Record your score on page 201.

Let's clear the air about slang. Slang's an excluding code consisting of invented words, for example "unfriend." Unfriend is a Facebook invention meaning to expunge someone from your friends' list. Facebook aficionados, a web sub group, grasp this code but outsiders can't. Yet Facebook is so popular, unfriend has entered the vernacular and gone from web slang to web jargon.

WPM Score =   **/ 60**

Review #10

Directions: You have 60 seconds to complete this task. Do not use a dictionary. Check your answers on page 192. Record your score on page 201.

1. vernacular (n)

a. mainstream language
b. native tongue
c. indigenous language
d. all of the above

2. adaptable (adj)

a. able to adapt
b. able to adjust
c. able to cope
d. all of the above

3. expediency (n)

a. palette
b. code
c. convenience
d. affordability

4. epiphany (n)

a. innate moment of realization
b. sudden revelation
c. personal discovery
d. all of the above

5. criteria (n)

a. list of rules used to judge
b. plural of criterion
c. points to follow when evaluating
d. all of the above

6. jargon (n)

a. form of slang
b. inclusive not exclusive code
c. code for special applications
d. all of the above

7. laissez-faire (phr)

a. closed-market business approach
b. free-market business model
c. foreign-market business style
d. all of the above

8. epitome (n)

a. quality
b. quintessence
c. epistle
d. underachiever

9. attribute to (v)

a. to give credit to
b. to acknowledge
c. to give benefit to
d. all of the above

10. salient (adj)

a. one that rises above the rest
b. one lower than the rest
c. one equal to all the rest
d. one harder than the rest

Extra Practice - A | Multiple-Choice Quiz

Directions: You have 8 minutes to complete this task. Do not use a dictionary. Check your answers on page 192. Record your score on page 201.

1. the blues (n)

a. black American music
b. early slave music
c. music expressing misery
d. all of the above

2. migrate (v)

a. to move in and around
b. to put down roots in a new land
c. to settle in an established place
d. all of the above

3. influence (n)

a. power to change
b. power to persuade
c. ability to bring about
d. all of the above

4. manifold (adj)

a. few
b. some
c. many
d. one

5. spawn (v)

a. to give birth to
b. to give rise to
c. to originate from
d. all of the above

6. visit upon (v)

a. to force upon
b. to go and visit
c. to spend time with
d. to educate about

7. in and around (phr)

a. about
b. after
c. beyond
d. at the exact time

8. unsung (adj)

a. recognized
b. rewarded
c. unrecognized
d. acknowledged

9. immeasurable (adj)

a. can be measured
b. cannot be measured
c. will be measured
d. too small to measure

10. puppy love (n)

a. adolescent love
b. first love
c. infatuation
d. all of the above

11. run a tight ship (id, v)

a. to demonstrate discipline
b. to be very organized
c. to operate efficiently
d. all of the above

12. prioritize (v)

a. to do whenever convenient
b. to do in order of importance
c. to cancel and do later
d. to reorganize and proceed

13. delegate (v)

a. to control everything
b. to assign responsibility
c. to manage without concern
d. to peddle ideas

14. capitalize on (v)

a. to take advantage of
b. to put in the bank
c. to borrow with low interest
d. to take in a new direction

15. break something down (v)

a. to stop moving
b. to cross into new territory
c. to divide and study in detail
d. to destroy for research

16. innate (adj)

a. born with
b. born in
c. born without
d. born at

17. tackle (v)

a. to confront
b. to deal with
c. to solve
d. all of the above

18. potential (n/adj)

a. ability wasted
b. ability not yet demonstrated
c. ability employed
d. all of the above

19. unfailingly (adv)

a. always
b. sometimes
c. never
d. now and then

20. cogent (adj)

a. convincing
b. sound
c. compelling
d. all of the above

21. a real dog (id)

a. superior product
b. inferior product
c. expensive product
d. affordable product

22. as lazy as a dog (id, n)

a. slothful
b. lethargic
c. indolent
d. all of the above

23. dog days (id, n)

a. slow, hot days of mid summer
b. time when many dogs are born
c. festival celebrating dogs
d. time when dogs sleep

24. denote (v)

a. to mean literally
b. to destroy completely
c. to mix thoroughly
d. to take notes copiously

25. underachiever (n)

a. one who always succeeds
b. one who does not succeed
c. one who wants to succeed
d. one who avoids success

26. against all odds (id, adv)

a. with a propensity for winning
b. with a good chance of success
c. with little or no chance of success
d. with a tendency to gamble

27. the hair of the dog (id, n)

a. idiom of Brazilian origin
b. idiom of Mexican origin
c. idiom of Roman origin
d. idiom of German origin

28. lethargic (adj)

a. recycling energy
b. no energy
c. losing energy
d. full of energy

29. highly (adv)

a. well
b. maybe
c. good
d. nearly

30. pay homage to (v)

a. to pay respect to
b. to acknowledge
c. to recognize
d. all of the above

Extra Practice - B   Sentence-Completion Quiz

Directions: You have 15 minutes to complete this task. Check your answers on page 192. Record your score on page 201.

Word List	unsung • immeasurable • pay homage to • a real dog • cogent the blues • as lazy as a dog • denote • underachiever • spawn • highly • migrate • influence • manifold • visit upon • innate • in and around • break something down • dog days • tackle • potential • unfailingly • against all odds • the hair of the dog • lethargic • puppy love • run a tight ship • prioritize • delegate • capitalize on •

1. Every year on January 8, thousands of fans travel to Graceland in Memphis, Tennessee to _____ the King of Rock and Roll, Elvis Presley.

2. Newly-elected presidents must always _____ a plethora of problems left behind by the previous president.

3. A cataclysmic drought was _____ the people of the American mid west during the Great Depression.

4. Rinaldo and Angela finally decided to bite the bullet and _____ to France.

5. Harvey's company always makes a profit because he _____ .

6. When Carrie is in a quandary, she always _____ the problem _____ so she can _____ it more effectively.

7. Some are very good at _____ while others are less punctilious.

8. As a musical genre, _____ is arguably one of the most influential.

9. During the _____ of summer, Terri is what one would call a couch potato.

10. If Pavel's innovative new software had such _____ , why did his boss pull the plug on it?

11. When addressing his professors, Timothy is _____ polite.

12. Contrary to popular belief, Yan is not _____ . Quite the contrary, he is always burning the candle at both ends.

13. Sagarika is a _____ regarded music teacher in India.

14. Yumi is a notorious _____ . She eschews any kind of work.

15. Illiana is wary about buying another iPod owing to the fact that her first iPod was _____ .

16. _____ connotes innocence.

17. Young children are susceptible to being easily _____ .

18. Contrary to popular belief, neither Apple nor Microsoft invented the computer mouse or the folders-based desktop system. Those seminal achievements belong to Xerox, an _____ innovator in the world of personal computers.

19. A remedy for a hangover is the Roman tradition called _____ .

20. _____ , Yu Chen kept her eye on the prize and won the gold medal.

21. When Wei Wei had the flu, she felt really _____ .

22. When the laser printed first hit the market in 1977, it _____ many imitators.

23. Einstein's _____ on science is _____ .

24. Candice searched _____ the park for her wayward friend.

25. Gina always makes such _____ comments in class.

26. People who are persnickety find it difficult _____ .

27. The indigenous tribes of the Amazon have an _____ understanding of the jungle.

28. Famine _____ no food.

29. Beth _____ the situation by killing two birds with one stone.

30. Xerox produced _____ seminal computer products. Case in point: the world's first laser printer invented by Gary Starkweather in 1969.

Extra Practice - C | 3 X 60-Word Typing Tests

Directions: You have 1 minute to type each of following 60-word passages. Record your scores on page 201.

Test #1

How does Samir run such a tight ship at work? Let's break it down. First, he always prioritizes. Next, he is not afraid to delegate authority in order to maximize efficiency and to capitalize on each employee's innate ability to recognize and tackle any potential problem. In addition, Samir specializes in explaining complex data in memoranda that are unfailingly cogent.

Test #2

The word dog is highly versatile. Puppy love means first love. A real dog is something that doesn't perform as expected whereas an underdog is an underachiever who claims victory against all odds. Lazy as a dog denotes you're lethargic perhaps because it's the dog days of summer. The hair of the dog is a drink to remedy a hangover.

<u>Test #3</u>

Indeed, the influence of the blues is immeasurable. Born in the slave south, it expresses the manifold miseries visited upon the black man. In and around 1900, the blues migrated north to Chicago and New York where it spawned jazz and rock. Elvis, the Beatles, even Frank Sinatra paid homage to the unsung originators of a truly original musical genre.

More Practice

Change the Quiz Order

After you have recycled all 50 exercises, wait a few days, then redo the quizzes but in a different order, for example:

1. Spelling (Quiz #3)
   Typing (Quiz #4)
   Sentence-Completion (Quiz #2)
   Multiple-Choice (Quiz #1)

2. Sentence-Completion (Quiz #2)
   Typing (Quiz #4)
   Spelling (Quiz #3)
   Multiple-Choice (Quiz #1)

3. Typing (Quiz #4)
   Spelling (Quiz #3)
   Sentence-Completion (Quiz #2)
   Multiple-Choice (Quiz #1)

Change the Time

After you have recycled all 50 exercises, wait a few days, then redo the quizzes but with shorter completion times, for example:

Quiz #1: from 2 minutes to 1 minute

Quiz #2: from 5 minutes to 2 minutes

Quiz #3: from 10 seconds to spell each word, phrase and idiom to 5 seconds

Quiz #4: from 1 minute to 45 seconds to type 60 words

Writing Practice

For each word, phrase and idiom, write it using a sentence of your own. Try combining as many words, phrases and idioms as you can to form a paragraph.

Speaking Practice

For each word, phrase and idiom, use it in a spoken sentence of your own. Try combining as many words, phrases and idioms as you can to form a spoken paragraph that focuses on one subject.

Typing Strategies

Many test-takers own laptop computers. Laptops have touch sensitive keyboards which are fast and easy to use. This style of typing is called "touch typing." However, on test day you will not use a laptop computer. Instead, you will use a standard desktop computer and a standard Microsoft keyboard, such as the one below.

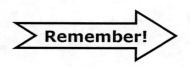 A standard keyboard is not touch sensitive. Also, because the distance between the letter keys and the function keys is greater on a standard keyboard, it takes more energy and focus to type quickly and accurately.

 Test center keyboards are often positioned low. This means you will have to extend your hands down to type. This is an unnatural position for laptop users.

 If you do not have a standard keyboard, it is recommend that you buy one and plug it into your laptop via the USB port. Standard keyboards are not expensive. As of this writing, you can buy one for $20.00 or less. A standard keyboard is definitely worth the investment.

The TOEFL Keyboard

A standard computer keyboard has 101 keys. For TOEFL, you will use only 48 of those keys. They are illustrated below.

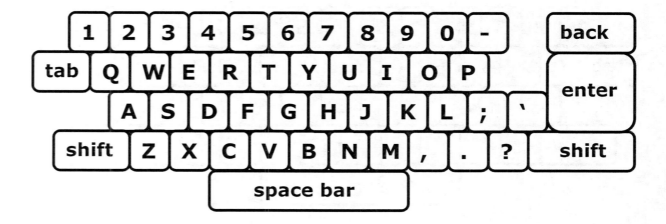

Home Row Keys

The most important row on the keyboard is the home row. There are 12 keys on the home row, including the enter key.

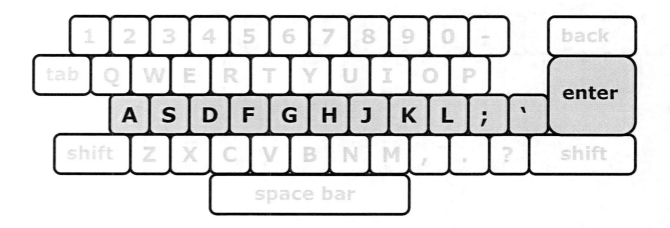

Top Row Keys

The two rows above the home row are called the top rows. They contain 23 keys.

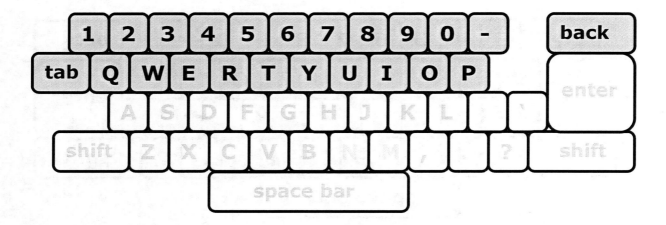

Bottom Row Keys

The bottom row contains 12 keys. <u>Note</u>: The question mark is a shift key (shift + question mark). Without the shift key, it is a forward slash key (/). For TOEFL, you will not use the forward slash key (/) only the question mark key.

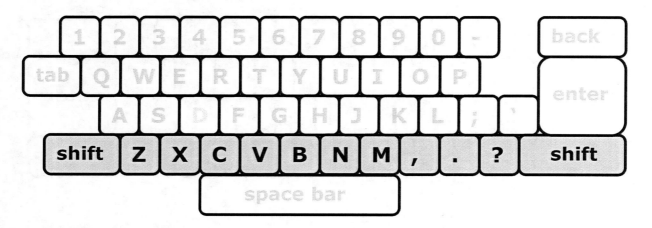

Finger Positioning

Each finger has a name. The names are the same for both hands.

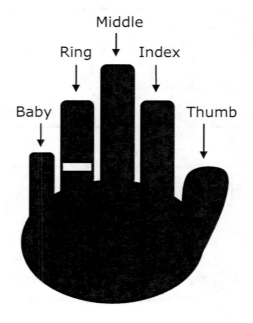

Left Hand – Baby Finger

Your left baby finger controls Z, A, Q, 1, shift, and tab.

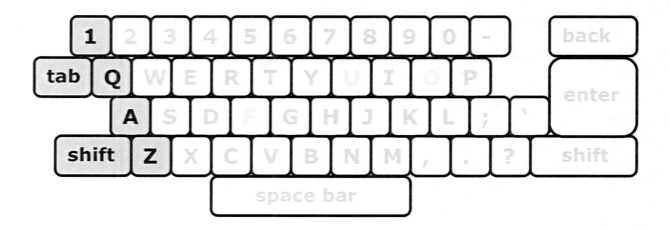

Left Hand – Ring Finger

Your left ring finger controls X, S, W, and 2.

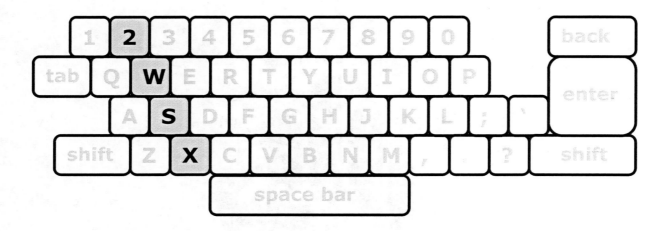

Left Hand – Middle Finger

Your left middle finger controls C, D, E, and 3.

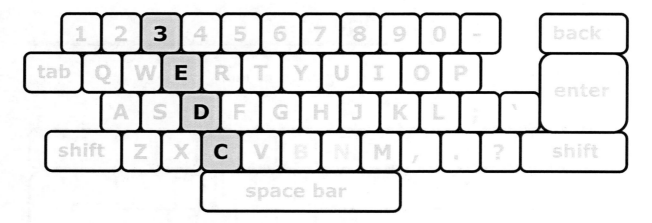

Left Hand – Index Finger

Your left index finger controls V, F, R, 4, B, G, T, 5, and 6.

Left Hand – Thumb

Your left thumb controls the space bar.

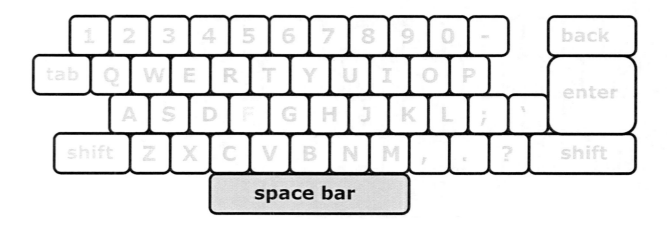

Right Hand – Baby Finger

Your right baby finger controls the question mark (?), the semi-colon (;), the apostrophe ('), P, O, the hyphen (-), back space, enter, and shift.

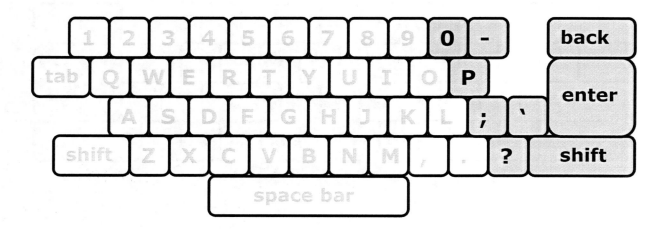

Right Hand – Ring Finger

Your right ring finger controls keys the period (.), L, O, and 9.

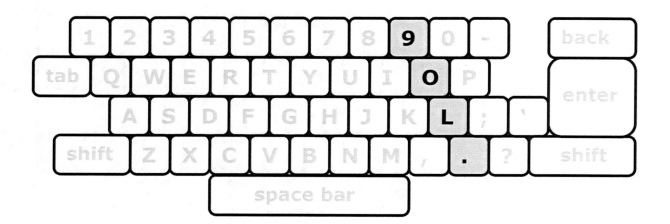

Right Hand – Middle Finger

Your right middle finger controls the comma (,), K, I, and 8.

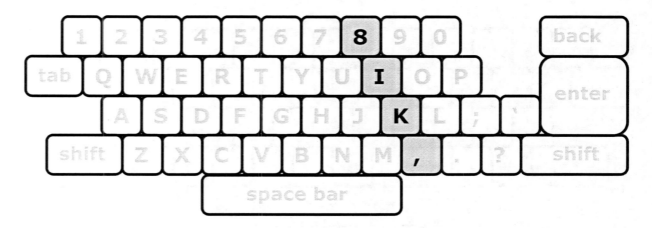

Right Hand – Index Finger

Your right index finger controls N, H, Y, 7, U, J, and M.

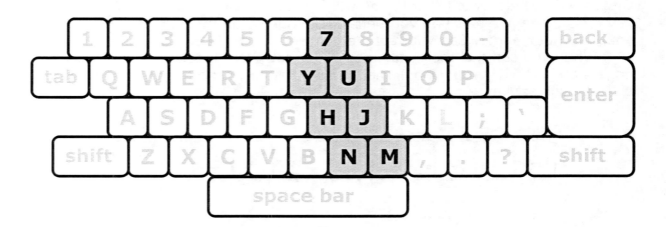

Right Hand – Thumb

Your right thumb controls the space bar.

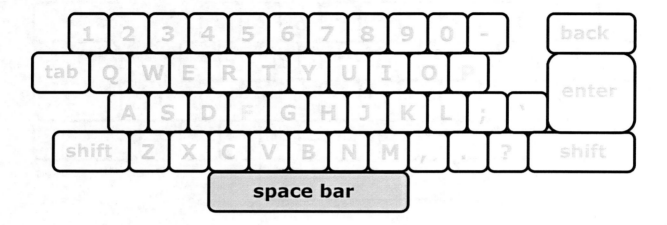

F and J Keys

F and J are the most important home row keys. Put your left index finger on F. On the F key, below the letter F, you will feel a small line sticking up from the key. This guide line tells you your left index finger is on the F key. Slowly rotate your left index finger. Can you feel the guide line? The J key also has a guide line. When you can feel the guide lines under both your index fingers, your index fingers are in the right position. That means that all your other fingers will be over the correct keys.

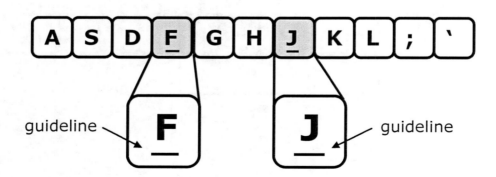

Ready Position

Place your fingers on the home row as illustrated below. This position is the ready position. For the greatest typing accuracy, each finger must start and return to this home row position after each key stroke.

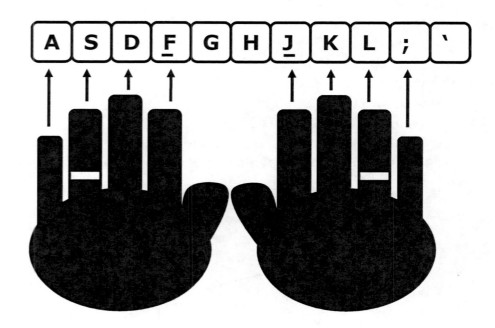

TASK: Put your hands in the ready position. Next, take your hands off. Without looking, put your fingers back on home row. Using the guide lines, locate the F key with your left index finger and the J key with your right index finger. Practice until you can position and reposition yours hands without looking.

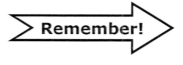 When you type, do not go fast. If you go fast, you will make more mistakes. Type at an average and consistent speed.

 Typing is a skill you will need at any English-speaking school and at work.

Ergonomics

Before you type, make sure you are sitting in the right position. Check each of the following. The right body position will increase typing speed and accuracy.

- Adjust the chair to the proper height.
- Relax and square your shoulders.
- Make sure the keyboard is at the right height; it should be level or a little higher than your waist.
- Make sure your back is straight and slightly forward.
- Make sure your forearms and hands form a continuous line.
- Make sure your wrists are straight.
- Make sure your feet are flat on the floor.
- Your eyes should be level with the top edge of the monitor; you should be looking slightly down at the screen so your chin is down.
- Place your fingers in the ready position.

Exercise A – Home Row Keys

Directions: For this exercise, start in the ready position and do the following for this exercise and for all exercises.

- ✓ Go slowly. Accuracy is more important than speed. Do not stop. Do not correct.
- ✓ Say each letter as you type it. Leave a space between each letter.
- ✓ Do not look at the keys. Instead, use the guide lines to find home row
- ✓ Repeat each line until every letter is correct. When finished, do the test.

```
ffffddddssssaaaajjjjkkkkllll;;;;''''ffffjjjj
aa''s s;;ddllffkkggjjaahhss''dd;;ffllggkka
f;ja'lks;a;sldkf'ghf;jad'ks;a;sldkf'ghfj' f
```

Vocabulary: Practice typing these home-row words.

```
has  had  as  lad's  fad  add  gas  hall  lag  gag  fall  dad's  sad  all  ad
```

Test #1: You have 60 seconds to type the following 60-word passage. Record your wpm score on page 204.

An argument that successfully persuades or informs demonstrates coherence. Coherence means that the argument is clear and logical. A coherent argument demonstrates English language proficiency. Proficiency means skill and knowledge. How can you construct personal-opinion and fact-based arguments that demonstrate coherence? By starting with a clear method of organization. There are two ways to organize an argument: deduction and induction.

Exercise B – Top Row Keys

Directions: For this exercise, follow the same directions as in Exercise A.

q q q q w w w w e e e e r r r r t t t t y y y y u u u u i i i i o o o o p p p

q p w o e i r u t y q p w o e i r u t y q p w o e i r u t y q p w o e i r u t

t y r u e i w o q p t y r u e i w o q p t y r u e i w o q p t y r u e i w o q

t q t w t e t r y u y i y o y p y t q t w t e t r y u y i y o y p y t q t w t e

---

1 2 3 4 5 6 7 8 9 0 t 0 9 8 7 6 5 4 3 2 1 2 3 4 5 6 7 8 9 0 t 1 2 3 4 y

q 1 w 2 e 3 r 4 t 5 t 6 y 7 I 8 o 9 p 0 q 1 w 2 e 3 r 4 t 5 t 6 u 7 I 8 y

1 0 2 9 3 8 4 7 5 y 6 1 0 2 9 3 8 4 7 5 y 6 1 0 2 9 3 8 4 7 5 y 6 t y 1

t e 9 3 5 7 3 w 2 0 3 u 9 3 5 7 3 3 3 5 y e u e e 2 9 1 0 0 9 9 e p e

---

Vocabulary: Practice typing these top-row words and numbers.

---

it to were up yet trip try wire top owe won prop too quite

now two pow write tote pop rip tot rot wit witty writ err

error rye yeti ire ore quit rube roti rete quiet wow trite two

one rote tie wrote rite route rout riot quote troupe quitter

weir ire trope twitter eye writer tip pip qwerty equerry

11 10 19 18 17 76 48 39 29 10 27 31 63 88 40 30 21

389 228 199 387 394 448 226 385 692 307 281 105 397

TEST #2: You have 60 seconds to type the following 60-word passage. Record your wpm score on page 204.

Body paragraph development is important because developing examples is the hardest part of the independent essay. Why is it the hardest part? Because body paragraph development will test your automaticity. Automaticity means your ability to develop ideas quickly and proficiently under a time pressure. Well-developed body paragraphs will demonstrate automaticity, proficiency and coherence. That is what the raters look for.

Exercise C – Bottom Row Keys

Directions: For this exercise, follow the same directions as in Exercise A.

z z z z x x x x c c c c v v v v b b b b n n n n m m m m , , . . ? ? z z z

b n v m c , x . z ? b n v m c , x . z ? b n v m c , x . z ? b n v m c , x

b v c x z n m , . ? ? ? ? b v c x z n m , , , , b v c x z n m . . . . . ? ?

v c , n z m c , z ? z c , x n v b z , n m c n x z . . z z c v x b , n b c z

Test #3: You have 60 seconds to type the following 60-word passage. Record your wpm score on page 204.

Americans assume that all business cultures are like theirs. Nothing could be further from the truth. For example, many Middle Eastern and Asian cultures prefer to do business face-to-face. Discussing business over tea or while having dinner is an integral part of the business process in these cultures. Such traditions help develop mutual respect and trust between international business partners.

Exercise D – Shift Keys

Directions: For this exercise, follow the same instructions as in Exercise A.

TOEFL iBT ETS CNN ITV ABC Globo CBS RCN XHDF BBC NHK

Microsoft Mitsubishi Apple Toyota Brahma Budweiser Versace

Fiat VW BMW Mercedes-Benz Vatican Paris Mecca Sao Paulo

Bogota Venezuela Beijing Seoul Cairo Tokyo Istanbul Madrid

Vocabulary: Practice typing these words.

I My The First Second Third Finally Lastly Personally Generally

This That There Those These They Therein At In But Yet

However Nevertheless Nonetheless Indeed Therefore If Hence

Inasmuch as Furthermore Another Indeed Because Since Albeit

TEST #4: You have 60 seconds to type the following 60-word passage. Record your wpm score on page 204.

An argument is the process of presenting an opinion for the purpose

of persuading. For TOEFL, this type of argument is called a personal-

opinion argument. An argument, however, doesn't always have to

persuade. An argument can also inform by presenting facts. For

TOEFL, this argument's called a fact-based argument. An argument

that successfully persuades or informs demonstrates coherence.

Exercise E – Back Space Key

The back space key is a function key used to delete letters, words, and spaces. When using the back space key, use your left ring finger or left baby finger.

Directions: In the following exercise, each word is spelled incorrectly. Type the word as it appears below, then correct the spelling using the back space key.

TOELF Amerika coffeee Windowz Mississippee Cali4nia thier

ferst secund lastlee teasis ohpinion arquement esamplez

furdermore cohearance especial additinally teecher estudent

Manhatten dohlar Presidente brakefast boredroom aeroplane

hamberger computa mices unimpossible collectabill steaki heros

adress beggining expresso enviroment makeing geneology

Nikeys intresting vaquum writting espelling hight weerd potatoe

oppurtwonity sentance tounge lazer alot ain't gonna zeebra

TEST #5: You have 60 seconds to type the following 60-word passage. Record your wpm score on page 204.

If you want high speaking and writing scores, your personal-opinion arguments and your fact-based arguments must demonstrate coherence. Coherence means that the individual parts of your argument are working together proficiently to deliver a clear and logical message. For TOEFL, a coherent argument is a high-scoring argument. A coherent argument demonstrates English language proficiency. Proficiency means skill and knowledge.

The tab key is also a function key. It is used primarily for indenting. When you indent, you move the first sentence of a paragraph in five spaces. An indent signals the beginning of a new paragraph, as the following example illustrates.

> **indent** >
>   If you're like me, you love to share music with your friends by downloading it from their computers. This is not stealing music. Hardly. My friends and I are simply sharing songs. In fact, I share music with people all over the world, people I don't know and will never meet. This process is called P2P or peer-to-peer file sharing. Now think: Is sharing something that you love a crime? I don't think so.
>
> **indent** >
>   I really want to stress this point: what I do in the privacy of my home is nobody's business but my own. Period. I don't need the government telling me what I can or can't do with my computer. The United States is a democracy not a dictatorship.

Indenting is a paper-based writing style. For TOEFL, you can indent your essays or you can use block-style. Block-style is an internet-based writing style.

> **block** >
> If you're like me, you love to share music with your friends by downloading it from their computers. This is not stealing music. Hardly. My friends and I are simply sharing songs. In fact, I share music with people all over the world, people I don't know and will never meet. This process is called P2P or peer-to-peer file sharing. Now think: Is sharing something that you love a crime? I don't think so.
>
> **block** >
> I really want to stress this point: what I do in the privacy of my home is nobody's business but my own. Period. I don't need the government telling me what I can or can't do with my computer. The United States is a democracy not a dictatorship.

Return Key

The return key has two functions: to enter information and to advance a line. Every time you hit enter, a line is added to your document, as indicated by the paragraph markers in the example below. To delete a line, hit the back space key as many times as needed.

 **Remember!** Paragraph markers (¶) indicate the end of a line. They are invisible and work in the background.

 **paragraph markers**

> If you're like me, you love to share music with your friends by downloading it from their computers. This is not stealing music. Hardly. My friends and I are simply sharing songs. In fact, I share music with people all over the world, people I don't know and will never meet. This process is called P2P or peer-to-peer file sharing. Now think: Is sharing something that you love a crime? I don't think so.¶
> ¶
> ¶
> ¶
> I really want to stress this point: what I do in the privacy of my home is nobody's business but my own. Period. I don't need the government telling me what I can or can't do with my computer. The United States is a democracy not a dictatorship.¶
> ¶

Remember! The enter key is also used for entering information. For TOEFL, the information you will enter into the computer, such as answering multiple-choice questions or moving between screen pages, is done primarily with a mouse.

Extra Exercises

Directions: For this exercise, type all four lines continuously. Go slowly and say each letter as you type it. Remember to return to the ready position after you type each letter.

```
A q Z s W x M e c F r v g T B hy n j u m k i , l o . ; P ? g H t y b N t y
t B y n R v u M e c I , w X O . q z p ? t b Y Q r v u m E c i , w x o . q
6 n 7 b 5 m 8 v 4 , 9 C 3 . 0 x 1 ? 6 n 7 b 5 m 8 v 4 , 9 c 3 . 0 x 1 ?
G r 9 3 i e A i A 2 c n , S a ; o e o 3 i 7 3 6 7 3 w n Z ? w ? 4 0 a G i
```

TEST #6: You have 60 seconds to type the following 60-word passage. Record your wpm score on page 204.

The American Civil War was fought between the northern and the

southern states from 1861 to 1865. A total of 618,000 soldiers died.

More soldiers died in the American Civil War than in all of America's

wars combined, from the Revolutionary War right on up to the Iraq

War. The Civil War started when the South withdrew from the Union.

Answer Key

Exercise 1-A (p. 4)

1. b
2. c
3. b
4. a
5. d
6. c
7. d
8. a
9. a
10. b

Exercise 1-B (p. 5)

1. astounding
2. species
3. camouflage
4. diurnal
5. prey on
6. accelerates
7. resolute
8. carnivore
9. attained
10. eschews

Exercise 2-A (p. 7)

1. a
2. d
3. b
4. b
5. c
6. d
7. b
8. d
9. a
10. d

Exercise 2-B (p. 8)

1. thesis
2. coherent
3. distractor
4. Proficiency
5. selective tasks
6. constructive tasks
7. intelligible
8. integral part of
9. holistic
10. rated

Exercise 3-A (p. 10)

1. a
2. d
3. c
4. c
5. a
6. d
7. d
8. b
9. a
10. c

Exercise 3-B (p. 11)

1. emancipated
2. fertile
3. exhausting
4. chaotic
5. transformation
6. assiduous
7. undergo
8. reliable
9. prosper
10. agrarian

Exercise 4-A (p. 13)

1. b
2. a
3. d
4. d
5. d
6. d
7. d
8. a
9. d
10. d

Exercise 4-B (p. 14)

1. trailblazer
2. merge, merged, merging
3. fundamental
4. innovative
5. inasmuch as
6. envisaged
7. wary
8. germinated
9. vulnerable
10. versatile

Exercise 5-A (p. 16)

1. d
2. d
3. b
4. d
5. d
6. a
7. a
8. b
9. d
10. d

Exercise 5-B (p. 17)

1. analogous
2. abundance
3. connotes
4. domestic
5. indeed
6. dissimilar
7. a plethora of
8. a myriad of
9. quite
10. alludes to

Review #1 (p. 19)

1. c
2. a
3. b
4. c
5. d
6. d
7. d
8. d
9. a
10. d

Exercise 6-A (p. 20)

1. a
2. d
3. d
4. d
5. d
6. c
7. a
8. d
9. d
10. b

Exercise 6-B (p. 21)

1. thaw
2. keen
3. harbinger
4. perch
5. inferred
6. offspring
7. precarious
8. quest
9. brood
10. profuse

Exercise 7-A (p. 23)

1. b
2. d
3. d
4. c
5. a
6. c
7. d
8. c
9. a
10. d

Exercise 7-B (p. 24)

1. quite the contrary
2. impecunious
3. All in all
4. subsist on
5. to reimburse
6. Suffice it to say
7. benevolent
8. inveterate
9. insinuated
10. judicious

Exercise 8-A (p. 26)

1. a
2. a
3. b
4. d
5. d
6. d
7. b
8. b
9. d
10. c

Exercise 8-B (p. 27)

1. posthumously
2. palette
3. unerring
4. towering
5. shimmering
6. snubbed
7. mercurial
8. hues
9. saturated
10. masterpiece

Exercise 9-A (p. 29)

1. a
2. b
3. c
4. d
5. a
6. c
7. a
8. c
9. b
10. d

Exercise 9-B (p. 30)

1. criminology
2. archeology
3. Climatology
4. meteorology
5. ology
6. geology
7. discombobulated
8. psychology
9. Sociology
10. anthropology

Exercise 10-A (p. 32)

1. d
2. d
3. a
4. d
5. d
6. a
7. b
8. d
9. c
10. d

Exercise 10-B (p. 33)

1. contrivances
2. novel
3. opulent
4. environs
5. per capita
6. Spartan
7. dwellings
8. void of
9. inhabit
10. renounced...renounce

Review #2 (p. 35)

1. d
2. d
3. a
4. a
5. a
6. a
7. d
8. a
9. a
10. d

Exercise 11-A (p. 36)

1. d
2. a
3. a
4. a
5. d
6. c
7. d
8. b
9. b
10. b

Exercise 11-B (p. 37)

1. drought
2. destitute
3. Precipitation
4. downfall
5. omen
6. render
7. abandon
8. famine
9. arable
10. arid

Exercise 12-A (p. 39)

1. c
2. d
3. c
4. b
5. d
6. d
7. b
8. a
9. c
10. d

Exercise 12-B (p. 40)

1. widespread
2. turbulent
3. to repeal
4. unquenchable
5. reigned

6. corruption
7. notorious
8. ruthless
9. nefarious
10. pervaded

Exercise 13-A (p. 42)

1. d
2. a
3. b
4. d
5. d
6. b
7. d
8. c
9. b
10. a

Exercise 13-B (p. 43)

1. landscape
2. sweeps through
3. deadliest
4. shatter
5. Avalanches
6. tsunami
7. disaster
8. tornados
9. placid
10. hurricane

Exercise 14-A (p. 45)

1. d
2. b
3. b
4. d
5. d
6. d
7. d
8. d
9. d
10. a

Exercise 14-B (p. 46)

1. turn a profit
2. target market
3. aggregate
4. to acquire
5. shares...shares
6. turn...around
7. profited
8. conglomerate
9. go bankrupt
10. to take over

Exercise 15-A (p. 48)

1. d
2. d
3. a
4. d
5. c
6. d
7. d
8. a
9. b
10. d

Exercise 15-B (p. 49)

1. irreplaceable
2. quadrupeds
3. endangered
4. extinct
5. primate
6. habitat...vanishing
7. DNA
8. vanished
9. herbivore
10. primarily

Review #3 (p. 51)

1. a
2. a
3. d
4. b
5. b
6. b
7. b
8. d
9. d
10. c

Exercise 16-A (p. 52)

1. d
2. a
3. a
4. a
5. a
6. a
7. d
8. c
9. a
10. d

Exercise 16-B (p. 53)

1. galaxy
2. Black holes
3. cosmos
4. cataclysmic
5. dinosaurs

6. orbiting
7. wiping out
8. asteroids
9. meteor
10. comet

Exercise 17-A (p. 55)

1. d
2. d
3. d
4. d
5. d
6. d
7. d
8. d
9. d
10. d

Exercise 17-B (p. 56)

1. ravenous
2. diligent
3. miraculous
4. copious
5. Ous
6. comestibles
7. On top of that
8. punctilious
9. superfluous
10. ludicrous

Exercise 18-A (p. 58)

1. d
2. a
3. d
4. a
5. d
6. c
7. d
8. d
9. c
10. d

Exercise 18-B (p. 59)

1. Chloroplast
2. unique
3. atmosphere
4. to capture
5. to convert
6. photosynthesis
7. whereby
8. organisms
9. to absorb
10. molecule

Exercise 19-A (p. 61)

1. d
2. b
3. c
4. a
5. c
6. d
7. d
8. c
9. a
10. c

Exercise 19-B (p. 62)

1. anathema
2. antipathy
3. abolitionist
4. proposition
5. immoral/anathema
6. labeled
7. precipitated
8. secession
9. ceased
10. enflamed...antipathy

Exercise 20-A (p. 64)

1. a
2. b
3. d
4. a
5. b
6. d
7. a
8. d
9. d
10. c

Exercise 20-B (p. 65)

1. exchange
2. devastating
3. indigenous
4. monumental
5. launches
6. flourishing
7. heretofore
8. hence...monumental
9. immunity
10. era

Review #4 (p. 67)

1. d
2. d
3. a
4. d
5. c

6. c
7. d
8. c
9. d
10. a

Exercise 21-A (p. 68)

1. d
2. d
3. d
4. d
5. d
6. d
7. a
8. d
9. d
10. d

Exercise 21-B (p. 69)

1. benefits
2. Catch-22
3. It goes without saying
4. pulled the plug
5. perplexed
6. dropped out of
7. persisting with
8. countered
9. quandary
10. enumerated

Exercise 22-A (p. 71)

1. c
2. d
3. b
4. d
5. c
6. c
7. d
8. b
9. a
10. a

Exercise 22-B (p. 72)

1. blown away
2. killed two birds with one stone
3. overwhelmed
4. painstaking
5. loaded
6. significant other
7. walking on air
8. gratis
9. pulled through with flying colors
10. The icing on the cake

Exercise 23-A (p. 74)

1. d
2. c
3. d
4. b
5. d
6. d
7. c
8. b
9. b
10. d

Exercise 23-B (p. 75)

1. misgivings
2. truly
3. regard
4. to overcome
5. esteemed
6. takes the bull by the horns
7. to pack it in
8. cherished
9. there and then
10. feel like a fish out of water

Exercise 24-A (p. 77)

1. b
2. d
3. d
4. b
5. c
6. d
7. a
8. d
9. a
10. d

Exercise 24-B (p. 78)

1. tion
2. address
3. the $64,000.00 question
4. reincarnation
5. contemplation
6. manifestation
7. disintegration
8. expiration
9. transfiguration
10. figment

Exercise 25-A (p. 80)

1. a
2. d
3. c
4. a
5. a
6. a
7. c
8. d
9. d
10. c

Exercise 25-B (p. 81)

1. The early bird gets the worm
2. espouses
3. resilient
4. without a doubt
5. the captain of her own ship
6. has her ducks in a row
7. climbing the corporate ladder
8. black and white
9. adage
10. indefatigable

Review #5 (p. 83)

1. d
2. d
3. c
4. d
5. d
6. d
7. a
8. d
9. c
10. c

Exercise 26-A (p. 84)

1. d
2. c
3. a
4. c
5. b
6. a
7. d
8. d
9. a
10. d

Exercise 26-B (p. 85)

1. contract
2. breached
3. stipulated
4. remedy
5. got wind of the fact that
6. recourse
7. apoplectic...got wind of the fact that
8. jurisdiction
9. negligent
10. Suing/To sue

Exercise 27-A (p. 87)

1. c
2. b
3. a
4. a
5. d
6. d
7. d
8. a
9. b
10. a

Exercise 27-B (p. 88)

1. ism
2. genius
3. affordable
4. Essentially
5. seminal
6. mass production
7. mass consumption
8. assembly line
9. substantially
10. mechanized

Exercise 28-A (p. 90)

1. a
2. b
3. d
4. a
5. d
6. b
7. c
8. c
9. d
10. a

Exercise 28-B (p. 91)

1. poultry
2. Pandemic
3. virulent
4. epidemic...pandemic
5. fatigued
6. strains
7. symptoms
8. transmitted
9. infectious
10. originated in

Exercise 29-A (p. 93)

1. d
2. a
3. b
4. b
5. d
6. b
7. c
8. d
9. d
10. a

Exercise 29-B (p. 94)

1. Symbol
2. owing to the fact that
3. susceptible
4. behemoth
5. tragic
6. doomed
7. indomitable
8. frigid
9. coalesce
10. perished

Exercise 30-A (p. 96)

1. a
2. d
3. c
4. d
5. a
6. b
7. b
8. d
9. d
10. a

Exercise 30-B (p. 97)

1. taken root
2. crucibles
3. founder
4. arguably
5. garages
6. genesis
7. inventiveness
8. incorporate
9. Moreover
10. iconic

Review #6 (p. 99)

1. a
2. b

3. a
4. d
5. d
6. d
7. a
8. d
9. a
10. d

Exercise 31-A (p. 100)

1. d
2. c
3. c
4. d
5. c
6. a
7. d
8. d
9. a
10. a

Exercise 31-B (p. 101)

1. none more so than
2. frontier
3. quintessential
4. self-reliant
5. archetypal
6. sublime
7. Rugged
8. herd
9. jack-of-all-trades
10. savaged

Exercise 32-A (p. 103)

1. d
2. c
3. b
4. d
5. a
6. b
7. a
8. d
9. b
10. c

Exercise 32-B (p. 104)

1. pod
2. life span
3. orcas
4. apex predator
5. Contrary to popular belief
6. matrilineal
7. resident
8. appellation

9. transient
10. stocky

Exercise 33-A (p. 106)

1. a
2. d
3. d
4. d
5. a
6. a
7. b
8. a
9. c
10. d

Exercise 33-B (p. 107)

1. assassinated
2. venerates
3. ratify
4. Absolute
5. confounded
6. apace
7. saint
8. archbishop
9. tyrannical
10. martyr

Exercise 34-A (p. 109)

1. a
2. c
3. a
4. b
5. d
6. b
7. d
8. d
9. a
10. c

Exercise 34-B (p. 110)

1. came with the territory
2. push the envelope
3. R & R
4. conviction
5. put her nose to the grindstone
6. burning the candle at both ends
7. aced
8. kicks back
9. to keep his eye on the prize
10. give….your best shot

Exercise 35-A (p. 112)

1. a
2. d
3. d
4. b
5. a
6. c
7. c
8. d
9. d
10. c

Exercise 35-B (p. 113)

1. ic
2. diehard
3. romantic
4. pragmatic
5. his feet on the ground
6. very much the
7. had their heads in the clouds
8. cynic
9. what one would call
10. enigmatic

Review #7 (p. 115)

1. d
2. b
3. d
4. a
5. d
6. a
7. b
8. a
9. d
10. c

Exercise 36-A (p. 116)

1. d
2. a
3. a
4. d
5. d
6. a
7. d
8. d
9. a
10. b

Exercise 36-B (p. 117)

1. parasitic
2. advent of… advent of
3. emblematic
4. boom

5. wayward
6. wholesale
7. brazen
8. malefactions
9. concurrent with
10. specious

Exercise 37-A (p. 119)

1. a
2. d
3. a
4. c
5. d
6. d
7. a
8. b
9. d
10. d

Exercise 37-B (p. 120)

1. double-edged sword
2. produce...organic
3. pesticides
4. purports
5. organic
6. cost an arm and a leg
7. trendy
8. taken her place in the spotlight
9. unadulterated
10. Nevertheless

Exercise 38-A (p. 122)

1. a
2. b
3. a
4. d
5. a
6. a
7. d
8. c
9. d
10. d

Exercise 38-B (p. 123)

1. wounded
2. bite the bullet
3. germs
4. evolved
5. primitive
6. surgery
7. amputation
8. rampant
9. antiseptic
10. anesthetic

Exercise 39-A (p. 125)

1. d
2. b
3. d
4. d
5. d
6. a
7. b
8. a
9. b
10. d

Exercise 39-B (p. 126)

1. persnickety
2. bent out of shape
3. ascertained
4. sort
5. infringements
6. multitude
7. accumulate
8. crossed the Rubicon
9. Neanderthal
10. transgression

Exercise 40-A (p. 128)

1. a
2. d
3. b
4. d
5. c
6. d
7. a
8. d
9. d
10. d

Exercise 40-B (p. 129)

1. immunity
2. nausea
3. fever
4. Mosquitoes
5. tropical
6. ensure
7. toxic
8. jaundiced
9. viruses
10. incubation

Review #8 (p. 131)

1. d
2. d
3. a
4. a
5. d

6. d
7. d
8. a
9. b
10. b

Exercise 41-A (p. 132)

1. b
2. a
3. b
4. c
5. d
6. d
7. a
8. d
9. d
10. d

Exercise 41-B (p. 133)

1. feral
2. litter
3. invasive
4. propensity... sustenance
5. hybrid
6. sustenance
7. deemed
8. cross
9. prodigious
10. harbored

Exercise 42-A (p. 135)

1. d
2. a
3. d
4. a
5. d
6. a
7. d
8. d
9. a
10. b

Exercise 42-B (p. 136)

1. elements
2. evaporate
3. hydrosphere
4. combust
5. decay
6. geosphere
7. pedosphere
8. eruption
9. Respiration
10. biosphere

Exercise 43-A (p. 138)

1. a
2. d
3. a
4. d
5. b
6. b
7. c
8. c
9. d
10. c

Exercise 43-B (p. 139)

1. post...War, post...War
2. chef
3. passion
4. gourmands
5. culinary
6. despises
7. chagrin
8. accomplished
9. Case in point
10. ground-breaking

Exercise 44-A (p. 141)

1. a
2. d
3. b
4. d
5. b
6. d
7. a
8. b
9. d
10. d

Exercise 44-B (p. 142)

1. countenance
2. obtuse
3. diffident
4. albeit
5. ebullient
6. nailed
7. inscrutable
8. disconcerted
9. insurmountable...
   inscrutable....or
   inscrutable...
   insurmountable
10. conundrum

Exercise 45-A (p. 144)

1. b
2. c
3. d
4. d
5. d
6. c
7. a
8. b
9. c
10. d

Exercise 45-B (p. 145)

1. entrepreneur
2. all manner of
3. infamous
4. expand her horizons
5. budding
6. rake in
7. Take no prisoners
8. peddle
9. widget
10. resurrect

Review #9 (p. 147)

1. b
2. d
3. d
4. d
5. c
6. d
7. a
8. b
9. b
10. b

Exercise 46-A (p. 148)

1. a
2. c
3. d
4. d
5. d
6. c
7. a
8. d
9. a
10. d

Exercise 46-B (p. 149)

1. employing
2. Stigmata
3. datum
4. Bacteria
5. peruse
6. dealt with
7. memoranda
8. criteria
9. salient
10. as in

Exercise 47-A (p. 151)

1. c
2. d
3. c
4. d
5. c
6. d
7. c
8. d
9. a
10. b

Exercise 47-B (p. 152)

1. hand in
2. mince words
3. ersatz
4. boon
5. epiphany
6. expediency
7. expunge
8. disingenuous
9. bevy of
10. endemic

Exercise 48-A (p. 154)

1. d
2. b
3. b
4. b
5. d
6. d
7. a
8. c
9. c
10. b

Exercise 48-B (p. 155)

1. zenith
2. resplendent
3. Impugning
4. harangue
5. epitome
6. impervious
7. equanimity
8. zenith...placate
9. laissez-faire
10. Rancor

Exercise 49-A (p. 157)

1. b
2. c
3. a
4. c
5. c
6. c

7. d
8. b
9. b
10. d

Exercise 49-B (p. 158)

1. target
2. patrol
3. voracious
4. adaptable
5. murky
6. attribute...to
7. unpredictable
8. testosterone
9. fatalities
10. territorial

Exercise 50-A (p. 160)

1. d
2. b
3. c
4. c
5. d
6. d
7. d
8. b
9. b
10. d

Exercise 50-B (p. 161)

1. aficionado
2. jargon
3. grasping
4. Grasping vernacular
5. gang
6. code
7. invention
8. clear the air
9. excised
10. excluding code

Review #10 (p. 163)

1. d
2. d
3. c
4. d
5. d
6. d
7. b
8. b
9. d
10. a

Extra Practice - A (p. 164)

1. d
2. b
3. d
4. c
5. d
6. a
7. a
8. c
9. b
10. d
11. d
12. b
13. b
14. a
15. c
16. a
17. d
18. b
19. a
20. d
21. b
22. d
23. a
24. a
25. b
26. c
27. c
28. b
29. a
30. d

Extra Practice - B (p. 167)

1. pay homage to
2. tackle/prioritize
3. visited upon
4. migrate
5. runs a tight ship
6. breaks...down...tackle
7. prioritizing
8. the blues
9. dog days
10. potential
11 unfailingly
12. as lazy as a dog
13. highly
14. underachiever
15. a real dog
16. Puppy love
17. influenced
18. unsung
19. the hair of the dog
20. Against all odds
21. lethargic
22. spawned

23. influence...
    immeasurable
24. in and around
25. cogent
26. to delegate
27. innate
28. denotes
29. capitalized on
30. manifold

Scores

Diagnostic Typing Test	/ 60 wpm		Exercise 7-A	/ 10
			Exercise 7-B	/ 10
Exercise 1-A	/ 10		Exercise 7-C	/ 10
Exercise 1-B	/ 10		Exercise 7-D	/ 60 wpm
Exercise 1-C	/ 10			
Exercise 1-D	/ 60 wpm		Exercise 8-A	/ 10
			Exercise 8-B	/ 10
Exercise 2-A	/ 10		Exercise 8-C	/ 10
Exercise 2-B	/ 10		Exercise 8-D	/ 60 wpm
Exercise 2-C	/ 10			
Exercise 2-D	/ 60 wpm		Exercise 9-A	/ 10
			Exercise 9-B	/ 10
Exercise 3-A	/ 10		Exercise 9-C	/ 10
Exercise 3-B	/ 10		Exercise 9-D	/ 60 wpm
Exercise 3-C	/ 10			
Exercise 3-D	/ 60 wpm		Exercise 10-A	/ 10
			Exercise 10-B	/ 10
Exercise 4-A	/ 10		Exercise 10-C	/ 10
Exercise 4-B	/ 10		Exercise 10-D	/ 60 wpm
Exercise 4-C	/ 10			
Exercise 4-D	/ 60 wpm		**Review #2**	/ 10
Exercise 5-A	/ 10		Exercise 11-A	/ 10
Exercise 5-B	/ 10		Exercise 11-B	/ 10
Exercise 5-C	/ 10		Exercise 11-C	/ 10
Exercise 5-D	/ 60 wpm		Exercise 11-D	/ 60 wpm
Review #1	/ 10		Exercise 12-A	/ 10
			Exercise 12-B	/ 10
Exercise 6-A	/ 10		Exercise 12-C	/ 10
Exercise 6-B	/ 10		Exercise 12-D	/ 60 wpm
Exercise 6-C	/ 10			
Exercise 6-D	/ 60 wpm		Exercise 13-A	/ 10
			Exercise 13-B	/ 10
			Exercise 13-C	/ 10
			Exercise 13-D	/ 60 wpm

Exercise 14-A	/ 10	Exercise 21-A	/ 10
Exercise 14-B	/ 10	Exercise 21-B	/ 10
Exercise 14-C	/ 10	Exercise 21-C	/ 10
Exercise 14-D	/ 60 wpm	Exercise 21-D	/ 60 wpm
Exercise 15-A	/ 10	Exercise 22-A	/ 10
Exercise 15-B	/ 10	Exercise 22-B	/ 10
Exercise 15-C	/ 10	Exercise 22-C	/ 10
Exercise 15-D	/ 60 wpm	Exercise 22-D	/ 60 wpm
Review #3	/ 10	Exercise 23-A	/ 10
		Exercise 23-B	/ 10
Exercise 16-A	/ 10	Exercise 23-C	/ 10
Exercise 16-B	/ 10	Exercise 23-D	/ 60 wpm
Exercise 16-C	/ 10		
Exercise 16-D	/ 60 wpm	Exercise 24-A	/ 10
		Exercise 24-B	/ 10
Exercise 17-A	/ 10	Exercise 24-C	/ 10
Exercise 17-B	/ 10	Exercise 24-D	/ 60 wpm
Exercise 17-C	/ 10		
Exercise 17-D	/ 60 wpm	Exercise 25-A	/ 10
		Exercise 25-B	/ 10
Exercise 18-A	/ 10	Exercise 25-C	/ 10
Exercise 18-B	/ 10	Exercise 25-D	/ 60 wpm
Exercise 18-C	/ 10		
Exercise 18-D	/ 60 wpm	**Review #5**	/ 10
Exercise 19-A	/ 10	Exercise 26-A	/ 10
Exercise 19-B	/ 10	Exercise 26-B	/ 10
Exercise 19-C	/ 10	Exercise 26-C	/ 10
Exercise 19-D	/ 60 wpm	Exercise 26-D	/ 60 wpm
Exercise 20-A	/ 10	Exercise 27-A	/ 10
Exercise 20-B	/ 10	Exercise 27-B	/ 10
Exercise 20-C	/ 10	Exercise 27-C	/ 10
Exercise 20-D	/ 60 wpm	Exercise 27-D	/ 60 wpm
Review #4	/ 10		

Exercise 28-A	/ 10
Exercise 28-B	/ 10
Exercise 28-C	/ 10
Exercise 28-D	/ 60 wpm
Exercise 29-A	/ 10
Exercise 29-B	/ 10
Exercise 29-C	/ 10
Exercise 29-D	/ 60 wpm
Exercise 30-A	/ 10
Exercise 30-B	/ 10
Exercise 30-C	/ 10
Exercise 30-D	/ 60 wpm
Review #6	/ 10
Exercise 31-A	/ 10
Exercise 31-B	/ 10
Exercise 31-C	/ 10
Exercise 31-D	/ 60 wpm
Exercise 32-A	/ 10
Exercise 32-B	/ 10
Exercise 32-C	/ 10
Exercise 32-D	/ 60 wpm
Exercise 33-A	/ 10
Exercise 33-B	/ 10
Exercise 33-C	/ 10
Exercise 33-D	/ 60 wpm
Exercise 34-A	/ 10
Exercise 34-B	/ 10
Exercise 34-C	/ 10
Exercise 34-D	/ 60 wpm
Exercise 35-A	/ 10
Exercise 35-B	/ 10
Exercise 35-C	/ 10
Exercise 35-D	/ 60 wpm

Review #7	/ 10
Exercise 36-A	/ 10
Exercise 36-B	/ 10
Exercise 36-C	/ 10
Exercise 36-D	/ 60 wpm
Exercise 37-A	/ 10
Exercise 37-B	/ 10
Exercise 37-C	/ 10
Exercise 37-D	/ 60 wpm
Exercise 38-A	/ 10
Exercise 38-B	/ 10
Exercise 38-C	/ 10
Exercise 38-D	/ 60 wpm
Exercise 39-A	/ 10
Exercise 39-B	/ 10
Exercise 39-C	/ 10
Exercise 39-D	/ 60 wpm
Exercise 40-A	/ 10
Exercise 40-B	/ 10
Exercise 40-C	/ 10
Exercise 40-D	/ 60 wpm
Review #8	/ 10
Exercise 41-A	/ 10
Exercise 41-B	/ 10
Exercise 41-C	/ 10
Exercise 41-D	/ 60 wpm
Exercise 42-A	/ 10
Exercise 42-B	/ 10
Exercise 42-C	/ 10
Exercise 42-D	/ 60 wpm

Exercise 43-A	/ 10
Exercise 43-B	/ 10
Exercise 43-C	/ 10
Exercise 43-D	/ 60 wpm
Exercise 44-A	/ 10
Exercise 44-B	/ 10
Exercise 44-C	/ 10
Exercise 44-D	/ 60 wpm
Exercise 45-A	/ 10
Exercise 45-B	/ 10
Exercise 45-C	/ 10
Exercise 45-D	/ 60 wpm
Review #9	/ 10
Exercise 46-A	/ 10
Exercise 46-B	/ 10
Exercise 46-C	/ 10
Exercise 46-D	/ 60 wpm
Exercise 47-A	/ 10
Exercise 47-B	/ 10
Exercise 47-C	/ 10
Exercise 47-D	/ 60 wpm
Exercise 48-A	/ 10
Exercise 48-B	/ 10
Exercise 48-C	/ 10
Exercise 48-D	/ 60 wpm
Exercise 49-A	/ 10
Exercise 49-B	/ 10
Exercise 49-C	/ 10
Exercise 49-D	/ 60 wpm

Exercise 50-A	/ 10
Exercise 50-B	/ 10
Exercise 50-C	/ 10
Exercise 50-D	/ 60 wpm
Review #10	/ 10
Extra Practice-A	/ 30
Extra Practice-B	/ 30
Extra Practice-C	/ 60 wpm
	/ 60 wpm
	/ 60 wpm

Typing Tests

Test #1	/ 60
Test #2	/ 60
Test #3	/ 60
Test #4	/ 60
Test #5	/ 60
Test #6	/ 60

Bonus Material

Arguments and the TOEFL iBT

The TOEFL iBT consists of four test sections: reading, listening, speaking and writing. Because the reading and listening questions are all multiple-choice questions, they are called selective tasks. In contrast, the speaking and writing tasks are called constructive tasks. For TOEFL, to construct means to develop and deliver. What do you have to develop and deliver on test day? Six verbal arguments and two written arguments.

Why does ETS use arguments to test your ability to speak and write academic English? Because at an English-speaking university, you will construct personal-opinion arguments, both verbally (independent speaking tasks #1 and #2) and in writing (independent writing task). You will also listen to and summarize lectures. Lectures are fact-based arguments (integrated writing task; integrated speaking task #4 and #6). You will also read and summarize fact-based arguments (integrated writing task; integrated speaking tasks #4 and #6).

As you can see, ETS uses arguments to test your ability to speak and write English academically. Therefore, to get high speaking and writing scores on the TOEFL iBT, *you must know how to construct and summarize both personal-opinion and fact-based arguments, quickly and proficiently*. You can do so using the strategy called argument mapping. Argument mapping begins with a review of basic argument development.

What is an argument?

An argument is the process of presenting an opinion for the purpose of persuading an audience. For TOEFL, this type of argument is called a personal-opinion argument. An argument, however, does not always have to persuade. An argument can also inform by presenting facts. For TOEFL, this type of argument is called a fact-based argument. An argument that successfully persuades or informs demonstrates coherence. Coherence means that the argument is clear and logical. For TOEFL, a coherent argument is a high-scoring argument. A coherent argument demonstrates English language proficiency. Proficiency means skill and knowledge. How can you quickly and proficiently construct both personal-opinion and fact-based arguments that demonstrate coherence? By starting with a clear method of organization. There are two ways to organize an argument: deduction and induction. Let's start with the personal-opinion argument and deduction.

Personal-Opinion Argument: *Deduction*

Read the following dialogue.

Jane: Hi, Mary. How was California?

Mary: California was the best trip ever. I learned how to surf at Malibu. At first, I kept falling off, but I kept trying and soon I could do it. It was great. And the sights.

Jane: Tell me.

Mary: I visited Hollywood first, Disneyland next, and Catalina Island last. There is so much to see and do. I was exhausted. Did I tell you about Jack?

Jane: Jack?

Mary: I met him at Venice Beach. He's a movie producer. He's so handsome. As a matter of fact, we're having dinner tonight. Tomorrow, we're flying back to L.A. to get married!

Jane: Sounds like you had a good time.

Mary: I had a fabulous time.

This is just an everyday conversation, right? Right. It is also a personal-opinion argument. How do we know it is a personal-opinion argument? We know because Mary starts her argument by stating her opinion about California. An opinion is also called a general statement.

> <u>Mary</u>: California was the best trip ever = opinion (general statement)

Next, Mary supports her opinion with three examples. Examples are also called supporting illustrations. Notice how each supporting illustration develops a reason why "California was the best trip ever."

example #1 I learned how to surf at Malibu. At first, I kept falling off, but I kept trying and soon I could do it. It was great.

example #2 And the sights. I visited Hollywood first, Disneyland next, and Catalina Island last. There is so much to see and do. I was exhausted.

example #3 Did I tell you about Jack? I met him at Venice Beach. He's a movie producer. He's so handsome. As a matter of fact, we're having dinner tonight. Tomorrow, we're flying back to L.A. to get married!

Finally, Mary makes a conclusion based on her opinion and her examples.

Mary: I had a fabulous time = conclusion

Where did Mary have "a fabulous time"? In California, of course.

 When you make a conclusion based on your opinion and your supporting examples, you are using deduction as a method of organization.

By mapping out Mary's dialogue, we can see how she uses deduction as a method of organizing her personal-opinion argument. Note how the opinion is called general. Notice also how the examples are called specific.

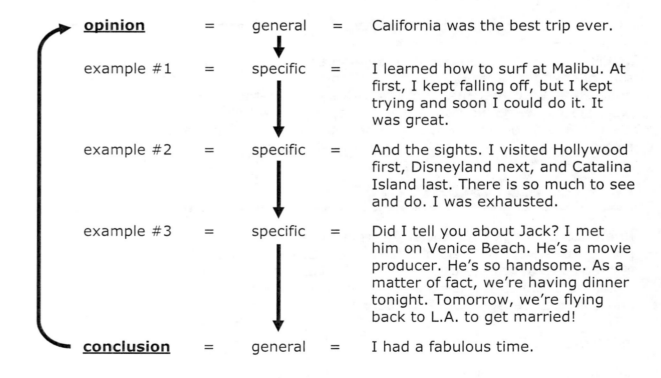

opinion	=	general	=	California was the best trip ever.
example #1	=	specific	=	I learned how to surf at Malibu. At first, I kept falling off, but I kept trying and soon I could do it. It was great.
example #2	=	specific	=	And the sights. I visited Hollywood first, Disneyland next, and Catalina Island last. There is so much to see and do. I was exhausted.
example #3	=	specific	=	Did I tell you about Jack? I met him on Venice Beach. He's a movie producer. He's so handsome. As a matter of fact, we're having dinner tonight. Tomorrow, we're flying back to L.A. to get married!
conclusion	=	general	=	I had a fabulous time.

Notice how Mary's **conclusion** confirms her **opinion** and takes us right back to the start. The speaking and writing raters will look for this closed or formal structure. Why? Because it shows that you are using deduction as a method of organizing your personal-opinion argument, be it written or verbal.

By adding **transitions** (connecting words), we can change Mary's verbal personal-opinion argument into a written personal-opinion argument.

California was the best trip ever.

For example, I learned how to surf at Malibu. At first, I kept falling off, but I kept trying and soon I could do it. It was great.

And the sights. I visited Hollywood first, Disneyland next, and Catalina Island last. There is so much to see and do. I was exhausted.

Also, did I tell you about Jack? I met him at Venice Beach. He's a movie producer. He's so handsome. As a matter of fact, we're having dinner tonight. Tomorrow, we're flying back to L.A. to get married!

In conclusion, I had a fabulous time.

TOEFL calls this written personal-opinion argument an independent essay. Yes, this independent essay is short and simple; nevertheless, it demonstrates coherence. Why? Because it starts with a clear method of organization in which Mary states her opinion about California, supports it with examples and reasons, then makes a conclusion based on her opinion and examples. Mary's argument also demonstrates a variety of rhetorical strategies.

Rhetorical Strategies

Rhetorical strategies are tools. A carpenter uses a hammer to build a house. A painter uses a brush to paint a landscape. Speakers and writers use rhetorical strategies to develop arguments. For TOEFL, you need to learn the following eight rhetorical strategies: narration, process, description, illustration, compare-and-contrast, cause-and-effect, definition, classification.

1. *Narration*

Narration describes the passing of time. When we arrange events according to time, we put them in chronological or time order, for example:

a.   Yesterday, Ann got up at seven o'clock and took a shower. After that she had breakfast, then rode the bus to work. When she got to work, she checked her email, then discussed the new business plan with her boss.

b.   Every Friday after class, Ellen goes to the gym and does yoga for three hours. When she is finished, she goes shopping, then takes the bus home.

2. *Process*

Process means putting events in sequential or step-by-step order. In the following examples, notice how each step-by-step process also describes the passing of time.

a.   When making tea, first boil water. Next, put a tea bag into a cup. When the water is boiling, pour the water into the cup. Finally, add milk and sugar as you prefer.

b.   *Titanic* hit an iceberg, broke in two, then sank.

3. *Description*

Description creates pictures of people, places and things using adjectives and adverbs. Description appeals to the senses: smell, sight, taste, hearing and touch.

a.   Alexander, the keyboard player in the band, is wearing a black leather jacket, faded jeans and red cowboy boots.

b.   The old man lived alone in an old house high on a rugged cliff overlooking a stormy sea.

4. *Illustration*

Illustration means example or supporting illustration, for example:

a.   There are many places to go for a honeymoon. For example, many newlyweds go to Hawaii.

b.   When you visit Manhattan, I suggest you visit Times Square and Central Park.

5. *Compare-and-Contrast*

Compare-and-contrast describes the differences and similarities between two or more objects, people or ideas. Compare-and-contrast also describes differences in opinion, for example:

a.   Raquel tried the apple pie and decided the cherry pie was sweeter.

b.   Ivan believes that all high school students should wear school uniforms; however, Paula believes that students should have the right to choose what they want to wear.

6. *Cause-and-Effect*

Cause-and-effect means action and result. We use cause-and-effect to describe an action and the results, or consequences, of that action, for example:

a.   Mohammed studied hard and got a high TOEFL score.

b.   Global warming is melting the ice at the North Pole.

7. *Definition*

A definition is a detailed description of a person, place, object or idea. The purpose of a definition is to give meaning, for example:

a.   The dodo was a flightless bird native to New Zealand.

b.   TOEFL is an English language proficiency test developed and implemented by Educational Testing Services (ETS) located in Princeton, New Jersey.

8. *Classification*

To classify means to put people, things or ideas into sub groups under a main topic, for example:

a.   There are three kinds of wine: red, white and rosé.

b.   TOEFL, TOEIC and IELTS are English language proficiency tests.

Now go back to Mary's argument. Look at the rhetorical strategies she uses to develop her examples. These, in turn, support her opinion and conclusion.

illustration → <u>places to visit</u>: Malibu Beach, Hollywood, Disneyland, Catalina Island, Venice Beach.
<u>things to do</u>: surfing, sightseeing, meeting guys (Jack).

description → <u>surfing at Malibu</u>: "It was great."
<u>after sightseeing</u>: "I was exhausted."
<u>Jack:</u> "He's so handsome."
<u>Jack</u>: "He's a movie producer."

process → <u>surfing</u>: "At first, I kept falling off, but I kept trying and soon I could do it."
<u>sightseeing</u>: I visited Hollywood first, Disneyland next, and Catalina Island last.

> **cause-effect**

surfing: "At first, I kept falling off (effect), but I kept trying (cause) and soon I could do it (effect)."
Jack: "I met him at Venice Beach." Go to Venice Beach and meet Jack (cause), fall in love (effect) and get married (cause).
Mary: She goes to California (cause) and her life changes completely (effect).
Jack: He visits Venice Beach (cause) and his life changes too (effect).

Personal-Opinion Argument: *Induction*

Induction is another way to organize a verbal or written personal-opinion argument. Look at the following examples. Notice how the deductive response begins with an opinion. In contrast, the inductive response develops three examples first, then ends with a conclusion (opinion) based on the examples.

Deduction	**Induction**
California was the best trip ever.	When I was in California, I learned how to surf at Malibu. At first, I kept falling off, but I kept trying, and soon I could do it. It was great.
I learned how to surf at Malibu. At first, I kept falling off, but I kept trying and soon I could do it. It was great.	
And the sights. I visited Hollywood first, Disneyland next, and Catalina Island last. There is so much to see and do. I was exhausted.	And the sights. I visited Hollywood first, Disneyland next, and Catalina Island last. There is so much to see and do. I was exhausted.
Did I tell you about Jack? I met him on Venice Beach. He's a movie producer. He's so handsome. As a matter of fact, we're having dinner tonight. Tomorrow, we're flying back to L.A. to get married!	Did I tell you about Jack? I met him at Venice Beach. He's a movie producer. He's so handsome. As a matter of fact, we're having dinner tonight. Tomorrow, we're flying back to L.A. to get married!
I had a fabulous time.	I had a fabulous time in California.

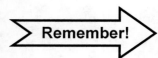 When you start a personal-opinion argument with examples—then make a conclusion based on your examples—you are using induction as the method of organizing your argument.

Developing Your Opinion

The most important part of your personal-opinion argument is your opinion. An opinion is also called a thesis.

Q *Is my opinion also the main topic?*

A *No. Look at the two sentences below.*

A.	I think California was the best trip ever.
B.	I think California was the worst trip ever.

In sentence A, the test-taker will write (or speak) about California. California, therefore, is the main topic (also called the main idea or main subject). The test-taker's opinion is "...*was the best trip ever.*" In sentence B, the test-taker will also write (or speak) about California. California is the main topic once again. However, the test-taker's opinion is "...*was the worst trip ever.*" As you can see, the main topic (California) is the same in both sentences; however, each sentence expresses a different opinion about California (best trip v. worst trip).

Q *How do I know if a sentence is an opinion or not?*

A *By asking these five questions.*

1.	Is it a complete sentence?
2.	Is it arguable?
3.	Is it supportable?
4.	Is it a question or not?
5.	Does it express one idea?

Mary said, "California was the best trip ever." That's her opinion. But how do we know it is an opinion without guessing? By asking the five questions.

1. | Is it a complete sentence?

Yes. The sentence "California was the best trip ever" is grammatically complete with a clear subject and verb tense.

2. | Is it arguable?

Yes. Mary has obviously considered her other vacations and concluded that California was the best compared to the rest. Where were her other vacations? We do not know. They are implied.

3. | Is it supportable?

Yes. Mary supports her opinion with three examples: 1) learning how to surf at Malibu; 2) going sightseeing; 3) meeting Jack.

4. | Is it a question or not?

Mary's opinion is not a question. An opinion is <u>never</u> a question.

5. | Does it express one idea?

Yes. Mary focuses on one main idea: having a fantastic time in California.

Based on the five questions, is the sentence "California was the best trip ever" an opinion? Yes.

What is not an opinion?

You now know what an opinion is, and how to identify one. So what is not an opinion? Follow these four rules.

1. An opinion is not a statement of fact.

a. *California is a big state.*

  This is not an opinion. This is a fact. It is not arguable.

b. *Californian red wine is the best in the world.*

> This is an opinion. It is a complete sentence, arguable, supportable, not a question, and expresses one idea.

2. <u>An opinion is not a question.</u>

a. *Is global warming a problem?*

> This is not an opinion. This is a question.

b. *Global warming threatens the future of the planet.*

> This is an opinion. It is a complete sentence, arguable, supportable, not a question, and expresses one idea.

3. <u>An opinion is not a fragment.</u>

a. *Paris: a great city.*

> This is not an opinion. It is not a complete sentence. It is a fragment. It is missing the verb "is."

b. *Without a doubt, Paris is the greatest city in the world.*

> This is an opinion. It is a complete sentence, arguable, supportable, not a question, and expresses one idea.

4. <u>An opinion does not simply announce the topic you will argue.</u>

a. *In this essay, I will talk about the problem of teenagers drinking and driving in my country.*

> This not an opinion. This test-taker is simply announcing (telling the reader) what he/she will write/speak about.

b. *Personally, I think that teenagers must finish high school before they can get a driver's license.*

> This is an opinion. It is a complete sentence, arguable, supportable, not a question, and expresses one idea.

Fact-Based Argument: *Deduction*

For TOEFL, you must also construct fact-based verbal and written arguments. A fact-based argument does not state a personal opinion. Instead, a fact-based argument begins by stating a general truth or fact called a premise. Look at the following example.

Rice is classified according to grain size.

First is long grain rice. An example is basmati. It is long and slender. When cooked, it becomes light and fluffy with the grains separating. Long grain rice is low in starch.

Next is medium grain rice. An example is Calrose. This type of rice is three times as long as it is wide. When cooked, the grains stick together. Medium grain rice has more starch than long grain rice.

Finally, there is short grain rice. An example is Arborio. It is kernel-shaped and becomes very moist and tender when cooked. Short grain has the highest starch level.

As illustrated, rice is classified according to grain size.

Notice how this fact-based argument uses deduction as the method organization. However, instead of starting with an opinion, it begins with a premise or general statement.

Rice is classified according to grain size = premise (general statement)

Note how the premise is supported by three supporting illustrations. Notice also how each supporting illustration develops and supports the fact that "Rice is classified according to grain size."

example #1 First is long grain rice. An example is basmati. It is long and slender. When cooked, it becomes light and fluffy with the grains separating. Long grain rice is low in starch.

example #2 Next is medium grain rice. An example is Calrose. This type of rice is three times as long as it is wide. When cooked, the grains stick together. Medium grain rice has more starch than long grain rice.

example #3   Finally, there is short grain rice. An example is Arborio. It is kernel-shaped and becomes very moist and tender when cooked. Short grain has the highest starch level.

Finally, the writer (or speaker) makes a conclusion based on the premise supported by the three examples. Note that the conclusion is simply the restated premise.

As illustrated, rice is classified according to grain size = conclusion

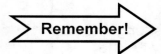 In a fact-based argument, when you make a conclusion based on the premise and supporting examples, you are using deduction as a method of organization.

By mapping out this fact-based argument, we can see how the writer (or speaker) is using deduction as a method of organizing his/her argument.

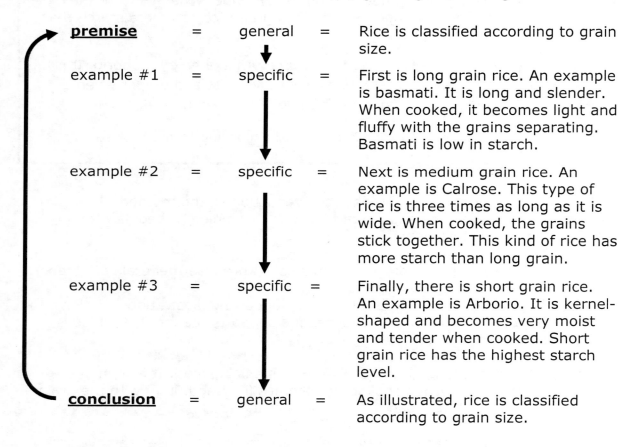

premise = general = Rice is classified according to grain size.

example #1 = specific = First is long grain rice. An example is basmati. It is long and slender. When cooked, it becomes light and fluffy with the grains separating. Basmati is low in starch.

example #2 = specific = Next is medium grain rice. An example is Calrose. This type of rice is three times as long as it is wide. When cooked, the grains stick together. This kind of rice has more starch than long grain.

example #3 = specific = Finally, there is short grain rice. An example is Arborio. It is kernel-shaped and becomes very moist and tender when cooked. Short grain rice has the highest starch level.

conclusion = general = As illustrated, rice is classified according to grain size.

Fact-Based Argument: *Induction*

You can also organize a verbal or written fact-based argument using induction. Look at the following examples. Notice how the deductive response begins with a premise. In contrast, the inductive response develops three examples first, then ends with a conclusion based on the examples.

Deduction	Induction
Rice is classified according to grain size. First is long grain rice. An example is basmati. It is long and slender. When cooked, it becomes light and fluffy with the grains separating. Long grain rice is low in starch. Next is medium grain rice. An example is Calrose. This type of rice is three times as long as it is wide. When cooked, the grains stick together. Medium grain rice has more starch than long grain rice. Finally, there is short grain rice. An example is Arborio. It is kernel-shaped and becomes very moist and tender when cooked. Short grain has the highest starch level. As illustrated, rice is classified according to grain size.	Basmati is an example of a long grain rice. It is long and slender. When cooked, it becomes light and fluffy with the grains separating. Long grain rice is low in starch. Next is Calrose, a medium grain rice. This type of rice is three times as long as it is wide. When cooked, the grains stick together. Medium grain rice has more starch than long grain rice. Finally, there is short grain rice. An example is Arborio. It is kernel-shaped and becomes very moist and tender when cooked. Short grain has the highest starch level. As illustrated, rice is classified according to grain size.

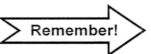
Remember! When you start a fact-based argument with examples—then make a conclusion based on your examples—you are using induction as the method of organizing your argument.

Coherence = A High Score

If you want high speaking and writing scores, your personal-opinion arguments and fact-based arguments must demonstrate coherence. Coherence means that the individual parts of your argument are working together proficiently to deliver a clear and logical message. An example is Mary's personal-opinion argument about California and the fact-based argument about rice. The message in both the deductive and inductive responses is clear: Mary had a fabulous time in California and rice is classified according to grain size. How can you make sure that your verbal and written arguments demonstrate coherence on test day? By using the strategy called argument mapping.

Argument Mapping

Argument mapping is a graphics-based strategy designed to help you map out the structure of personal-opinion and fact-based arguments quickly and proficiently. By doing so, both essay types will demonstrate coherence.

An understanding of argument mapping begins with the paragraph map <u>G+TiC</u>. Translated, <u>G+TiC</u> means:

General statement + **T**ransition + **i**llustration + **C**onclusion

<u>G+TiC</u> describes the three-parts of a paragraph.

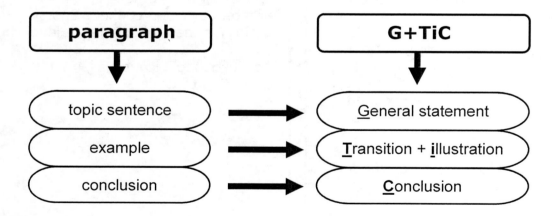

By adding two more body paragraphs (2TiC) and a conclusion (<u>C</u> = restated opinion or premise), <u>G+TiC</u> expands to <u>G+3TiC=C</u>.

G+3TiC=C

G+3TiC=C maps out a three-part personal-opinion argument and a three-part fact-based argument that uses deduction as a method of organization.

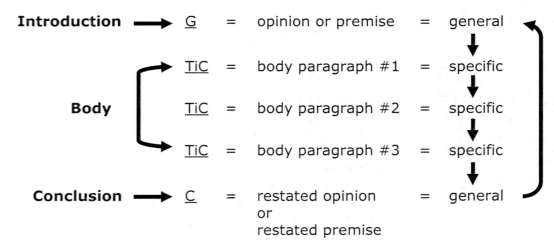

Introduction ⟶ G = opinion or premise = general

        TiC = body paragraph #1 = specific

Body   TiC = body paragraph #2 = specific

        TiC = body paragraph #3 = specific

Conclusion ⟶ C = restated opinion = general
or
restated premise

 **Remember!** Depending on the task, the general statement will either be your opinion (personal-opinion argument) or a premise (fact-based argument) supported by illustrations and a conclusion.

general statement + illustrations = conclusion

G + 3TiC = C

Q *Why three supporting illustrations?*

A *G+3TiC=C is based on the five-paragraph essay. The five-paragraph essay consists of an introduction, three body paragraphs and a conclusion. The five-paragraph essay is the foundation essay taught in American high schools. American high school students learn the five-paragraph essay and continue to apply it, and expand upon it, at community college and at university.*

Let's map out Mary's personal-opinion argument about California using <u>G+3TiC=C</u>. The opinion and conclusions are <u>underlined</u>, the transitions in **bold**, the *illustrations* in italics. Note that the general statement (G) is an opinion.

<u>G</u>   =   general   =   Personally, <u>I think California was the best trip ever</u>.

<u>TiC</u>   =   specific   =   **For example**, *I learned how to surf at Malibu. At first, I kept falling off, but I kept trying, and soon I could do it.* <u>It was great</u>.

<u>TiC</u>   =   specific   =   **And the sights.** *I visited Hollywood first, Disneyland next, and Catalina Island last. There is so much to see and do.* <u>I was exhausted</u>.

<u>TiC</u>   =   specific   =   **Also**, *did I tell you about Jack? I met him on Venice Beach. He's a movie producer. He's so handsome. As a matter of fact, we're having dinner tonight.* <u>Tomorrow, we're flying back to L.A. to get married</u>!

<u>C</u>   =   general   =   **In conclusion**, <u>I had a fabulous time</u>.

To map out the inductive response, delete Mary's opinion. This inductive argument map is <u>3TiC=C</u>. Notice how the first sentence in body paragraph one introduces the **context** or situation, and how the conclusion (C) is Mary's opinion based on her supporting illustrations (3TiC).

<u>TiC</u>   =   specific   =   ***When I was in California***, *I learned how to surf at Malibu. At first, I kept falling off, but I kept trying, and soon I could do it.* <u>It was great</u>.

<u>TiC</u>   =   specific   =   **And the sights!** *I visited Hollywood first, Disneyland next, and Catalina Island last. There is so much to see and do.* <u>I was exhausted</u>.

<u>TiC</u>   =   specific   =   **Also**, *did I tell you about Jack? I met him on Venice Beach. He's a movie producer. He's so handsome. As a matter of fact, we're having dinner tonight.* <u>Tomorrow, we're flying back to L.A. to get married</u>!

<u>C</u>   =   general   =   **In conclusion**, <u>I had a fabulous time in California</u>.

Next, let's map out the fact-based argument about rice using G+3TiC=C. The premise and conclusions are <u>underlined</u>, the transitions in **bold**, the *illustrations* in italics. Note that the general statement (G) is a premise.

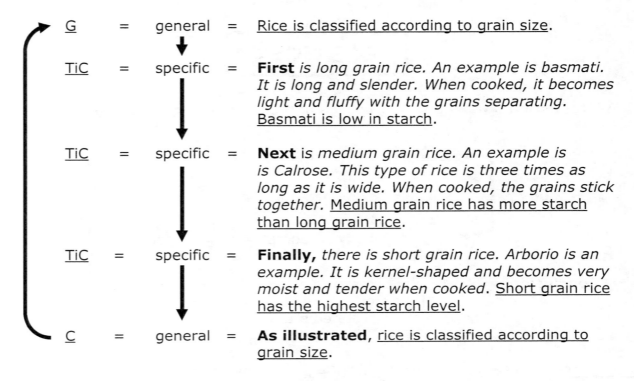

G	=	general	=	<u>Rice is classified according to grain size.</u>
TiC	=	specific	=	**First** *is long grain rice. An example is basmati. It is long and slender. When cooked, it becomes light and fluffy with the grains separating.* <u>Basmati is low in starch</u>.
TiC	=	specific	=	**Next** *is medium grain rice. An example is is Calrose. This type of rice is three times as long as it is wide. When cooked, the grains stick together.* <u>Medium grain rice has more starch than long grain rice.</u>
TiC	=	specific	=	**Finally,** *there is short grain rice. Arborio is an example. It is kernel-shaped and becomes very moist and tender when cooked.* <u>Short grain rice has the highest starch level.</u>
C	=	general	=	**As illustrated**, <u>rice is classified according to grain size.</u>

To map out the inductive response (3TiC=C), start with an example. Notice how the conclusion (C) is a premise based on the supporting illustrations (3TiC).

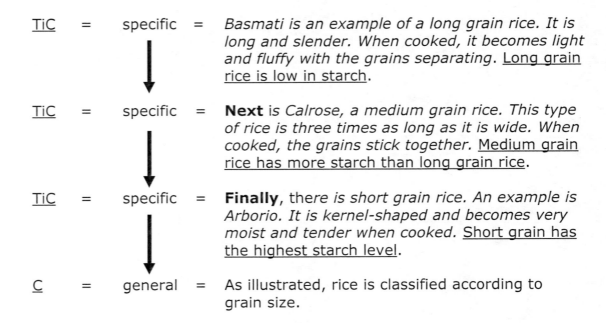

TiC	=	specific	=	*Basmati is an example of a long grain rice. It is long and slender. When cooked, it becomes light and fluffy with the grains separating.* <u>Long grain rice is low in starch.</u>
TiC	=	specific	=	**Next** *is Calrose, a medium grain rice. This type of rice is three times as long as it is wide. When cooked, the grains stick together.* <u>Medium grain rice has more starch than long grain rice.</u>
TiC	=	specific	=	**Finally**, *there is short grain rice. An example is Arborio. It is kernel-shaped and becomes very moist and tender when cooked.* <u>Short grain has the highest starch level.</u>
C	=	general	=	As illustrated, rice is classified according to grain size.

 **Remember!** You can use <u>G+3TiC=C</u> to develop and deliver responses for all six speaking tasks and for both writing tasks. That's right: one strategy for eight tasks (six speaking, two writing)

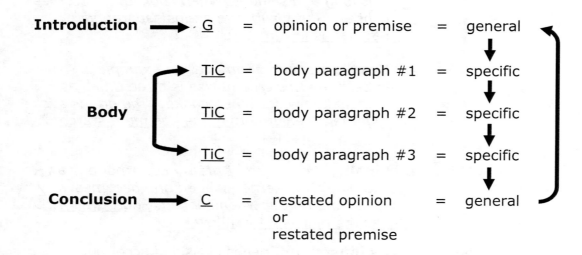

	G+3TiC=C			
Introduction →	<u>G</u>	=	opinion or premise	= general
Body	<u>TiC</u>	=	body paragraph #1	= specific
	<u>TiC</u>	=	body paragraph #2	= specific
	<u>TiC</u>	=	body paragraph #3	= specific
Conclusion →	<u>C</u>	=	restated opinion or restated premise	= general

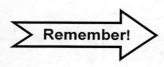 **Remember!** Learn more about <u>G+3TiC=C</u>® in *Speaking and Writing Strategies for the TOEFL iBT*. Available at Amazon.com and as a phone app. Visit www.argumentmapping.com and www.novapress.net for more.

TOEFL® iBT Facts

1. The TOEFL iBT is an English language proficiency test. TOEFL tests academic English language proficiency. For TOEFL, academic English means first year, college-level English.

2. TOEFL means "test of English as a foreign language." iBT means "internet-based test." Internet-based means the test computers are connected to the internet. Your answers will be sent via the internet to be scored by ETS.

3. The TOEFL iBT is designed and implemented by Educational Testing Services (ETS) Princeton, New Jersey, USA.

4. You cannot pass or fail the TOEFL test. You will get a score out of 120 total points. Your score measures your English language proficiency. The higher your score, the higher your English language proficiency.

5. The TOEFL iBT is divided into four test sections. You cannot change the task order.

Section	Task	Time	Score
Reading	3-5 essays	60-100 minutes	30/30
Listening	2-3 dialogues 4-6 lectures	60 minutes	30/30
	break	10 minutes	
Speaking	2 independent tasks 4 integrated tasks	2 minutes 18 minutes	30/30
Writing	1 integrated task 1 independent task	23 minutes 30 minutes	30/30
	Total:	4 hours	120/120

6. Before you take the TOEFL test, find out the TOEFL requirements of the school to which you are applying. Some U.S. colleges and universities do not require a TOEFL score.

7. In some countries, you can take the TOEFL PBT (paper-based test). If you want to go to graduate school in the United States, do not take the PBT. Take the iBT instead. Why? Because graduate and post graduate students at U.S. universities are expected to teach undergraduate classes. That means you must be able to speak academic English proficiently. That is what the iBT tests. The PBT does not test speaking.

8. In the United States, you can register for the TOEFL iBT online or by phone. Visit <u>www.ets.org</u> for registration information. In the United States, the busiest registration times are at the end of each school semester when TOEFL courses end and TOEFL students are ready to take the test. The TOEFL test is very popular. Register as early as possible.

9. You can take notes during the test. Pencils and paper will be supplied. You cannot use your own pencil or paper. After the test, you must give your notes to the test site manager.

10. Expect to use a standard Microsoft keyboard when you take the test.

11. Your TOEFL iBT score is good for two years. You cannot renew your TOEFL score. You must retake the test and get a new score. For more TOEFL information, visit <u>www.ets.org</u>.

Word List

The words in bold are the 500 words recycled through the 50 quizzes. The non bold words are words used in this text and are essential for TOEFL.

A

a myriad of
a piece of cake
a plethora of
a real dog
abandon
abide by
abode
abolitionist
abroad
absolute
absorb
abundance
abundant
accelerate
accomplished
accumulate
accuracy
ace
achieve
achievements
acknowledge
acquire
actualize
adage
adapt
adaptable
address
adequately
adjust
admission
advent of
advice
advocate
aerospace
affordability
affordable
aficionado
afterwards
against all odds

aggregate
agrarian
alarming
albeit
all in all
all manner of
allergic
allude to
alter
amalgam
ambiguity
ameliorate
amputation
analogous
anathema
ancient
anesthetic
angels
Antarctica
anthropology
antipathy
antiseptic
apace
apes
apex predator
apiology
apoplectic
appellation
appetite
approach
arable
arcane
archbishop
archeology
archetype
arguably
argue
argument
arid
army
as in
as you can see

ascertain
assassinate
assembly line
assiduous
assuage
assume
asteroid
astounding
astrology
atmosphere
atom
attain
attribute to
automaticity
avalanche
average

B

Baby Boom
bachelor
bacteria
bacterium
Bactrian
bait
bargain with
basic
battlefield
behemoth
benefits
benevolent
bent out of shape
bevy of
Big Foot
binding
biogeochemical cycle
biology
biosphere
biped
bite the bullet
black and white

black hole
blame
blow away
boar
bonds
boom
boon
bored
brainiac
brand
brazen
breach
**break something
 down**
brilliant
brood
budding
buffalo
bugs
**burn the candle at
 both ends**
bust
by accident

C

Caesar
call in sick
camouflage
cancer
canned
canonized
capitalize on
capture
carbohydrate
carbon
carcinogenic
carnivore
case in point
casualty
cataclysmic
Catch-22
cease
celestial
cement
ceramic
chagrin
challenging

champagne
championed
chaotic
chef
chemicals
cherish
chicanery
chin
chloroplast
chores
civilization
claim
clear the air about
climatology
climax
**climb the corporate
 ladder**
coalesce
cogent
coherent
coined by
colonial
Columbian Exchange
combust
comestible
comet
**come with the
 territory**
coherence
coherent
comforting
commence
complex
comprehensible
con
concurrent with
conditionally
conflict
confound
conglomerate
connote
conquer
consequently
consisting of
construct
constructive task
consuming
contagious

contemplation
contentment
continuous
contract
**contrary to popular
 belief**
contrivances
conundrum
convenience
convert
conviction
cope
copious
corporate tax
corruption
corrupts
cosmetology
cosmos
**cost an arm and a
 leg**
costly
couch potato
countenance
counter
court
crepuscular
criminology
criteria
criterion
critics
crop
cross
cross fertilize
cross the Rubicon
crucible
culinary
cut off
cyclonic
cynic

D

damage
data
dated
datum
dawn of time
deadliest

deal with
decay
deduction
deem
defeat
delegate
demand
demolished
denote
deny
dependent
despise
destined
destitute
determined
devastating
diehard
diffidence
diligent
dinosaurs
disaster
discombobulated
disconcerted
discovery
disingenuous
disintegration
dissimilar
dissolve
distractor
diurnal
divine
DNA
dog days
dolphins
domestic
doomed
dot.com bubble
double-edged
  sword
downfall
dream up
drenched
drop out of
drought
due to
duty
dwelling

E

ebullient
edible
educational
effectively
efficiency
election
element
elicit
emancipated
embarrassed
emblematic
emotion
employ
empty handed
endangered
endemic
energetic
enervating
enflame
enigmatic
ensure
entirely
entrepreneur
enumerate
environment
environs
envisage
epidemic
epiphany
epistle
epitome
equal
equanimity
equatorial
era
eradicate
ergonomics
ersatz
eruption
eschew
especially
espouse
essentially
evaporate
evolved
exacerbate

exactitude
examine
exchange
excise
excluding
exclusive
exhaustion
expand one's
  horizons
expansion
expediency
expiration
explosion
expression
expunge
extinct
extraordinary

F

faced with
factory
fake
famine
famished
fastidious
fatality
fatigue
fatuous
feasible
feel like a fish out
  of water
feral
fertile
fever
figment
fit in
fix it up
flicker
flourish
flu
focus
foes
for example
Fordism
foreign
forgery
formal

for the time being
fossil
fossil fuel
founder
frigid
frontier
frugal
frustrate
frustration
fundamental
furthermore
fussy

G

Galapagos
galaxy
gang
garage
generation
genesis
genetic
genius
genius
genre
geology
geosphere
germ
germinate
get out of
get out there
**get wind of the fact
that**
gigantic
give credit to
**give it one's best
shot**
go bankrupt
gorillas
gourmand
grant
grasp
gratis
Great Depression
Great White shark
grocery
ground-breaking
growth

H

habitat
hacker
hail
hand in
harangue
harbinger
harbor
**have both feet on
the ground**
**have one's ducks in
a row**
**have one's head in
the clouds**
hence
herbicide
herbivore
herd
heretofore
hibernate
hierarchy
highly
hit
holistic
holy
horrible
housewife
however
hue
hurricane
hybrid
hydrology
hydrosphere

I

ic
iconic
identity
ignore
illegal
imitators
immeasurable
immoral
immunity
impala
impecunious

impervious
imply
imposed
impugn
in addition
in and around
in contrast
in short
in the final analysis
in the wild
inasmuch as
include
inclusive
income tax rate
inconsiderate
incorporate
incubate
incubation
indeed
indefatigable
independent
indigenous
indomitable
induction
industrious
industry
infamous
infectious
infer
inferior
influence
influenza
infringement
inhabit
inhabitants
innate
innocent
innovate
inordinate
inscrutable
insect
insincere
insinuate
inspiration
inspired
insurmountable
integral part of
intellectual property

intelligible
interbreed
intercept
invasion
invasive
invention
inventiveness
invest
inveterate
ironically
irreplaceable
ism
issue
item
**it goes without
  saying**
Ivy League

J

jack-of-all-trades
jargon
jaundice
judge
judicious
Jurassic
jurisdiction
jury

K

keen
**keep one's eye on
  the prize**
kick back
**kill two birds with
  one stone**
knock off

L

label
lack
laissez-faire
landscape
launch
lawyer
lazy as a dog

legal
lethargic
life span
limb
litter
loaded
loathe
logic
logical
loyal
ludicrous
lunar
luxury

M

mainstream
majority
malefaction
mammals
manifestation
manifold
margin
martyr
marvelous
mass consumption
mass production
massive
masterpiece
matrilineal
matter
maximize
measurement
mechanized
memoranda
memorandum
memos
mend
mercurial
mercury
mercy
merge
Mesozoic
meteor
meteorology
micro processor
micro-organism
Middle Ages

migrate
Milky Way
mince words
miraculous
misgivings
molecule
mollify
monster
monumental
moreover
mortar
mosquito
multitude
murky
musicology

N

nadir
nail
namely
national debt
native
native to
nausea
Neanderthal
nefarious
negligent
negotiate
nerd
nevertheless
nocturnal
nomadic
none more so than
nonetheless
nonplused
notorious
nourishment
novel

O

obedient
obligation
obtuse
obvious
official
offspring

ology
omen
on top of that
opinion
opulent
orbit
orca
organic
organism
originate in
ous
outcome
outsiders
overcome
overdose
overfish
overshot
overwhelmed
owing to
owing to the fact
  that

P

pacific
pacify
pack it in
painstaking
palette
pandemic
parasite
parasitic
parliament
particle
particularly
pass on
passion
pathfinder
pathogen
patrilineal
patrol
pay homage to
peddle
pedosphere
penetrate
penguin
penurious
per capita

perch
perilous
perish
permission
perplexed
persist with
persnickety
perspiration
peruse
pervade
pesticide
pests
phase
phlegmatic
photosynthesis
physiology
piglets
pioneer
piracy
pity
placate
placid
planet
play ball
pod
point of no return
pole
polite
political
polluting
popularized
portable
post war
posthumously
potential
poultry
practical
pragmatic
precarious
precipitate
precipitation
predictable
predominantly
prescribe
prey on
primarily
primates
primitive

prioritize
prodigious
produce
proficiency
proficient
profit
profit
profuse
prohibit
Prohibition
promote
promptly
propensity
properly
property
property line
proposed
proposition
prosper
prosperity
prosperous
protein
psychology
public
pull the plug
pull through with
  flying colors
punctilious
puppy love
purport
push the envelope
put one's nose to
  the grindstone
put your stamp on
puzzlement

Q

quadruped
quandary
quest
quintessence
quintessential
quite
quite the contrary

R

R and R
rake in
rampant
rancor
rancorous
range
rapid
rapidly
rate
ratify
ravenous
realization
rebirth
recession
recourse
recycled
refined
regulate
reign
reimburse
reincarnation
reliable
rely on
remedy
remit
render
renounce
repeal
reputation
rescind
reside
resident
resilient
resolute
respiration
resplendent
responsibilities
restated
resurrect
retreat
reveal
revelation
revile
rhetoric
rhetorical
ridiculous

right at home
right on up to
rightful
rises
roll the dice
romantic
rugged
ruin
rule
run a tight ship
ruthless

S

saint
salary
salient
sasquatch
satellites
saturated
savage
seals
seasonal
secession
secondhand
seen as
seize
selective task
self-reliant
seminal
sequentially
set the price
severe
shallow
share
shark
shatter
shimmer
shun
significant
significant other
simultaneously
sincere
slightly
snub
soaked
social
sociology

solve
sophistication
sort
sow
Spartan
spawn
species
specious
spouse
spread
square
stagnant
starving
stigmata
stipulated
stock
stock market
stocky
stolid
strain
strict
stun
sub tropical
sublime
submit
subsist on
substantially
substitute
such as
sue
suffice it to say
superfluous
superior
surgeon
surgery
survive
susceptible
sustenance
sweep through
symbol
symptom
synonymous

T

tackle
take care of
take in

take no prisoners
take one's place in the spotlight
take over
take root
take the bull by the horns
tame
target
target market
tend to
tendency
territorial
territory
testosterone
thaw
the blues
the captain of one's own ship
the early bird gets the worm
theft
the hair of the dog
the icing on the cake
there and then
therein
thesis
the $64,000.00 question
tion
tiring
topic
tornado
tortoise
towering
toxic
track
tractor
tragic
trailblazer
transfiguration
transformation
transgression
transient
transition
transmit
treat

trendy
trespasser
tropical
try out
tsunami
turbulent
turn
turn around
typical
tyrannical
tyrant

U

unadulterated
unappeased
uncivilized
underachiever
underdog
undergo
undoubtedly
unerring
unfailingly
unfathomable
unfriend
unimaginably
unique
universe
unpredictable
unquenchable
unrealistic
unrepentant
unresolvable
unsung
unwillingly
utter

V

vaccine
vanish
vanquish
vegan
venerate
venture
verbal
vernacular
versatile

very much the
victorious
violation
virulent
virus
visit upon
void of
volcanic
voracious
voters
vulcanology
vulnerable

W

walk on air
wander
warm-blooded
wary
wayward
weakness
what one would call
when all is said and done
when everything is considered
whereas
whereby
wholesale
wicked
widespread
widget
wild
wipe out
wise
withdraw
without a doubt
worship
wounded

Y

yellow fever

Z

zebras
zenith

Also from *Nova Press*

Master the LSAT (608 pages; includes software and 4 official exams)

GMAT Prep Course (624 page; includes software and online course)

The MCAT Physics Book (444 pages)

The MCAT Chemistry Book (496 pages)

Speaking and Writing Strategies for the TOEFL iBT (398 pages; audio CD)

SAT Prep Course (640 pages; includes software)

Law School Basics: A Preview of Law School and Legal Reasoning (224 pages)

Vocabulary 4000: 4000 Words for an Educated Vocabulary (160 pages)

Nova Press
11659 Mayfield Avenue
Los Angeles, CA USA 90049
1-800-949-6175
info@novapress.net
www.novapress.net